CZECH REPUBLIC
TRAVEL GUIDES
2024

Hidden Gems and Historic Treasures: Your Ultimate Czech Adventure

RAPHA SMITH

Copyright © 2024 by RAPHA SMITH. All right reserved.

No part of this book may be reproduced or transmitted in any form or by any means, electronic or mechanical including photocopy, recording, or by any information storage and retrieval system without written permission from the author except for the inclusion of brief quotation in a review.

TABLE OF CONTENT

1.0 INTRODUCTION
1.1 OVERVIEW OF THE CZECH REPUBLIC
1.2 BRIEF HISTORY AND CULTURAL BACKGROUND OF THE CZECH REPUBLIC

2.0 GETTING STARTED
2 1 PLANNING YOUR TRIP TO THE CZECH REPUBLIC
2.2 VISA AND ENTRY REQUIREMENTS TO THE CZECH REPUBLIC: A DETAILED GUIDE
2.3 CURRENCY AND MONEY MATTERS IN THE CZECH REPUBLIC
2.4 LANGUAGE AND COMMUNICATION TIPS

3.0 DESTINATIONS
3.1 PRAGUE: A MAGNIFICENT CITY OF HISTORY AND CULTURE
- *3.1.1 Old Town Square: Prague's Historical Heart*
- *3.1.2 Prague Castle: A Majestic Symbol of Czech History and Culture*
- *3.1.3 Charles Bridge: A Timeless Icon Connecting Prague's History*

3.2 ČESKÝ KRUMLOV: A FAIRYTALE TOWN ALONG THE VLTAVA RIVER
3.3 KARLOVY VARY: A SPA TOWN OF ELEGANCE AND WELLNESS
3.4 BRNO: THE DYNAMIC HEART OF MORAVIA

3.5 PLZEŇ: WHERE BEER, HISTORY, AND CULTURE CONVERGE
3.6 KUTNÁ HORA: A MEDIEVAL GEM WITH GOTHIC SPLENDOR

4.0 TRANSPORTATION
4.1 GETTING TO THE CZECH REPUBLIC: YOUR GATEWAY TO CENTRAL EUROPE
4.2 LOCAL TRANSPORTATION
4.3 RENTING A CAR IN THE CZECH REPUBLIC: FREEDOM TO EXPLORE THE HEART OF EUROPE
4.4 PUBLIC TRANSPORT TIPS IN THE CZECH REPUBLIC

5.0 ACCOMMODATION

5.1 HOTELS AND RESORTS IN THE CZECH REPUBLIC
5.2 HOSTELS AND BUDGET ACCOMMODATIONS

6.0 CUISINE
6.1 TRADITIONAL CZECH DISHES: CULINARY DELIGHTS FROM THE HEART OF EUROPE
6.2 POPULAR RESTAURANTS AND CAFÉS IN THE CZECH REPUBLIC
6.3 FOOD FESTIVALS AND EVENTS IN THE CZECH REPUBLIC

7.0 CULTURAL EXPERIENCES
7.1 FESTIVALS AND CELEBRATIONS IN THE CZECH

REPUBLIC: A TAPESTRY OF CULTURE AND TRADITION
7.2 MUSEUM AND GALLERIES
7.3 HARMONY AND EXPRESSION: PERFORMING ARTS AND MUSIC IN THE CZECH REPUBLIC
7.4 LOCAL TRADITIONS AND CUSTOMS IN THE REPUBLIC

8.0 OUTDOOR ACTIVITIES
8.1 HIKING AND NATURE TRAILS
8.2 SKIING AND WINTER SPORTS
8.3 WATER ACTIVITIES
8.4 NATIONAL PARKS AND RESERVES

9.0 PRACTICAL TIPS
9.1 SAFETY AND EMERGENCY INFORMATION
9.2 HEALTH AND MEDICAL SERVICES

9.3 LOCAL ETIQUETTE AND CUSTOMS
9.4 SUSTAINABLE TRAVEL PRACTICES

10.0 USEFUL RESOURCES
10.1 ESSENTIAL APPS AND WEBSITES
10.2 RECOMMENDED GUIDEBOOKS
10.3 LOCAL TOURIST INFORMATION CENTERS

11.0 APPENDIX
11.1 GLOSSARY OF CZECH PHRASES
11.2 MAPS AND NAVIGATIONAL AIDS
11.3 WEATHER AND CLIMATE INFORMATION

1.0 INTRODUCTION

1.1 OVERVIEW OF THE CZECH REPUBLIC

The Czech Republic, located in the heart of Europe, is a landlocked country known for its rich history, captivating architecture, and vibrant culture. As of my last update in January 2022, let's delve into key aspects that contribute to the country's unique character.

Geography and Location:
Situated in Central Europe, the Czech Republic shares borders with Germany to the west, Austria to the south, Slovakia to the east, and Poland to the northeast. Its central location has historically made it a crossroads for trade and cultural exchange.

Capital and Major Cities:
Prague, often referred to as "the City of a Hundred Spires," serves as the capital and largest city of the Czech Republic. Known for its stunning medieval architecture and charming cobblestone streets, Prague is a UNESCO World Heritage Site. Other notable cities include Brno, Ostrava, and Plzeň.

Historical Significance:
Boasting a rich historical tapestry, the Czech Republic was once part of the Austro-Hungarian Empire and later the first Czechoslovak Republic after World War I. The peaceful Velvet Revolution of 1989 marked the end of communist rule, leading to the establishment of the independent Czech Republic in 1993 after the dissolution of Czechoslovakia.

Cultural Heritage:
The Czech Republic has made significant contributions to literature, music, and art. Renowned figures like Franz Kafka and Antonín

Dvořák hail from this region. The country's cultural landscape is dotted with castles, chateaux, and picturesque towns that reflect its diverse heritage.

Architectural Splendors:
Prague's Old Town Square, Charles Bridge, and Prague Castle showcase a blend of Gothic, Baroque, and Romanesque architecture. Beyond Prague, Český Krumlov, a UNESCO World Heritage Site, is famed for its well-preserved medieval architecture. Kutná Hora, with its unique Bone Church (Sedlec Ossuary), adds a macabre yet fascinating touch to the country's architectural wealth.

Economic Landscape:
Post-communism, the Czech Republic experienced robust economic growth, becoming one of the more developed and industrialized nations in Central Europe. Industries such as automotive manufacturing, technology, and tourism contribute significantly to the economy.

Natural Beauty:
The Czech Republic boasts diverse landscapes, from the Bohemian Forest to the picturesque Moravian vineyards. Outdoor enthusiasts can explore national parks like Šumava and Krkonoše, offering hiking, skiing, and other recreational activities.

Language and People:
Czech is the official language, and the majority of the population identifies as Czech. The people are known for their hospitality and cultural pride. English is commonly spoken in tourist areas, enhancing the travel experience for international visitors.

The Czech Republic's allure lies in its captivating blend of history, architecture, and cultural richness. Whether strolling through the charming streets of Prague or exploring the country's natural wonders, visitors are sure to be enchanted by the Czech Republic's multifaceted charm.

1.2 BRIEF HISTORY AND CULTURAL BACKGROUND OF THE CZECH REPUBLIC

Historical Tapestry:

The roots of the Czech Republic's history are intertwined with the broader narrative of Central Europe. The Czech lands were home to various Slavic tribes before the establishment of the Great Moravian Empire in the 9th century. However, it was under the rule of the Přemyslid dynasty in the 10th century that the foundations of the Czech state were laid.

Golden Age and Hussite Wars:
The 14th and 15th centuries marked a Golden Age for the Kingdom of Bohemia, with Prague becoming a significant cultural and economic hub of Europe. However, religious tensions erupted into the Hussite Wars in the 15th century, challenging the Catholic Church and leaving a lasting impact on the region's religious landscape.

Habsburg Rule and Austro-Hungarian Empire:
The Habsburgs came to power in the 16th century, incorporating Bohemia into their vast empire. The Czech lands became an integral part of the Austro-Hungarian Empire, enduring

periods of prosperity and suppression. The late 19th century witnessed a resurgence of Czech national identity, leading to the foundation of Czechoslovakia after World War I.

First Czechoslovak Republic:

The establishment of Czechoslovakia in 1918 marked a turning point. A democratic republic emerged, bringing together Czechs and Slovaks. Tomáš Garrigue Masaryk, the first president, played a pivotal role in shaping the nation's early years. This era witnessed cultural flourishing and economic development.

World War II and Communist Era:

Tragically, the country fell victim to Nazi occupation during World War II. Post-war, Czechoslovakia experienced a brief period of democracy, but the 1948 coup led to four decades of communist rule. The Prague Spring in 1968, a brief period of liberalization, was violently suppressed by the Soviet Union and its allies.

Velvet Revolution and Independence:
The late 20th century brought transformative change. The Velvet Revolution of 1989, led by figures like Václav Havel, marked the end of communist rule. Czechoslovakia transitioned to a democratic state, and in 1993, peacefully split into the Czech Republic and Slovakia.

Post-Communist Renaissance:
The post-communist era saw rapid economic development and integration into Western institutions. The Czech Republic became a member of the European Union in 2004, solidifying its place in the broader European community.

Cultural Richness:
Czech culture is a tapestry woven with influences from various historical periods. The country's literature, exemplified by figures like Franz Kafka and Milan Kundera, reflects both historical struggles and contemporary themes. Music is another cornerstone, with composers

such as Antonín Dvořák and Bedřich Smetana contributing to the global classical repertoire.

Architectural Legacy:
The architectural landscape mirrors the nation's history, featuring Gothic gems, Baroque splendors, and modernist structures. Prague Castle, Charles Bridge, and the Astronomical Clock stand as iconic symbols of the country's cultural and artistic heritage.

Festivals and Traditions:
Czechs celebrate a rich tapestry of festivals, from the vibrant Prague Carnival to the traditional Easter markets. Cultural traditions like the colorful Majáles festival and the lively Masopust carnival contribute to the country's festive spirit.

The Czech Republic's history is a story of resilience, cultural richness, and a continual quest for freedom. From medieval kingdoms to the Velvet Revolution, the nation's journey has shaped its unique identity, making it a captivating destination for those eager to explore the crossroads of Central European history and culture.

2.0 GETTING STARTED

2 1 PLANNING YOUR TRIP TO THE CZECH REPUBLIC

Planning a trip to the Czech Republic involves a series of exciting decisions and considerations to ensure a smooth and enjoyable experience. Here's a comprehensive guide to help you navigate the process:

1.Research and Destination Selection:
- Explore the diverse regions of the Czech Republic, including Prague, Bohemia,

Moravia, and picturesque towns like Český Krumlov.
- Consider the time of year you plan to visit, taking into account seasonal activities and events.

2. Travel Documents and Visa:
- Check visa requirements based on your nationality and the duration of your stay.
- Ensure your passport has sufficient validity and that you have all necessary travel documents.

3. Budgeting and Currency:
- Determine your travel budget, factoring in accommodation, transportation, meals, and activities.
- Familiarize yourself with the local currency (Czech Crown) and exchange rates.

4. Accommodation Booking:
- Explore a range of accommodation options, from hotels to hostels and Airbnb.
- Consider staying in various neighborhoods to experience different facets of the destination.

5. Transportation:
- Research transportation options to and within the Czech Republic, including flights, trains, and buses.
- Consider renting a car for more flexibility, especially if you plan to explore beyond major cities.

6. Language and Cultural Familiarity:
- Learn a few basic Czech phrases to enhance your travel experience.
- Familiarize yourself with local customs and etiquette to respect cultural norms.

7. Health and Travel Insurance:
- Check if you need any vaccinations before traveling.
- Consider obtaining travel insurance to cover unforeseen circumstances, including medical emergencies and trip cancellations.

8. Activities and Itinerary Planning:
- Identify key attractions and activities based on your interests.
- Create a flexible itinerary, allowing time for spontaneity and exploration.

9. Local Cuisine and Dining Reservations:
- Explore Czech cuisine and identify must-try dishes.
- Make reservations at popular restaurants, especially in peak tourist seasons.

10. Weather Considerations:
- Check the weather for the time of your visit and pack accordingly.

- Be prepared for seasonal variations, especially if you plan outdoor activities.

11. Local Transportation and Maps:
- Familiarize yourself with public transportation options within cities.
- Download offline maps or use navigation apps to ease exploration.

12. Cultural Events and Festivals:
- Check the calendar for cultural events and festivals taking place during your visit.
- Plan your trip to coincide with unique local celebrations for a richer experience.

13. Safety and Emergency Information:
- Research safety tips and emergency contact information.
- Stay informed about local customs to avoid potentially sensitive situations.

14. Pack Smartly:
- Pack versatile clothing suitable for various activities and weather conditions.

- Include essentials like adapters, chargers, and any specific items required for your planned activities.

15. Stay Connected:
- Consider purchasing a local SIM card or an international roaming plan to stay connected.
- Install relevant travel apps for navigation, translation, and local information.

By carefully planning each aspect of your trip, you can maximize your enjoyment of the Czech Republic, immersing yourself in its rich history, culture, and natural beauty.

2.2 VISA AND ENTRY REQUIREMENTS TO THE CZECH REPUBLIC: A DETAILED GUIDE

Before embarking on your journey to the Czech Republic, it's crucial to understand the visa and entry requirements to ensure a smooth and hassle-free entry into the country. As of my last update in January 2022, here's a comprehensive guide:

1. Visa Exemptions:
- Citizens of European Union (EU) countries and the European Economic Area (EEA) do not require a visa for short stays (up to 90 days within a 180-day period).

- Certain other nationalities, including the United States, Canada, Australia, and Japan, are visa-exempt for short stays.

2. Schengen Area Membership:
- The Czech Republic is a member of the Schengen Area, which means a Schengen visa allows entry into the Czech Republic along with other Schengen countries.

3. Short-Stay Schengen Visa:
- If you are not visa-exempt, you may need to apply for a short-stay Schengen visa for visits up to 90 days within a 180-day period.
- The visa is suitable for tourism, business, or family visits.

4. Application Process:
- Submit your visa application at the Czech embassy or consulate in your country of residence.
- Provide required documents, including a completed application form,

passport-sized photos, travel itinerary, proof of accommodation, travel insurance, and proof of financial means.

5. Long-Stay Visa and Residence Permit:
- For stays exceeding 90 days, a long-stay visa or residence permit is required.
- These visas are typically for purposes such as work, study, or family reunification.

6. Work and Residence Permits:
- If you plan to work in the Czech Republic, you will need a work permit and residence permit.
- Your employer may assist with the application process.

7. Student Visas:
- Students planning to study in the Czech Republic need a student visa.
- Admission to a recognized educational institution and proof of financial means are essential requirements.

8. Family Reunification:

- Family members of EU/EEA citizens may be eligible for family reunification without a visa.

Non-EU family members need a residence card issued by the Czech Republic.

9. Visa Fees and Processing Time:

- Visa fees vary based on the type and duration of the visa.
- Processing times also vary, so it's advisable to apply well in advance of your planned travel date.

10. Border Control and Entry Procedure:

- Even with a valid visa, border control authorities may ask for supporting documents upon entry.
- Ensure you have proof of accommodation, return ticket, and financial means available.

11. Health Insurance:
- Travelers are required to have travel insurance covering medical expenses for the entire duration of their stay.
- Health insurance must meet the Schengen requirements.

12. Biometric Data:
- As part of the visa application process, biometric data (fingerprints) may be collected.

13. Changes and Updates:
- Entry requirements and visa policies can change, so regularly check the official website of the Ministry of Foreign Affairs of the Czech Republic or the respective embassy/consulate for updates.

14. Overstaying and Penalties:
- Overstaying the allowed duration can result in fines, deportation, or future entry bans.
- Adhere strictly to the conditions of your visa to avoid legal complications.

15. Special Circumstances:
- Check for any special circumstances or exemptions that may apply to your specific situation.
- Consular officers have discretion in certain cases.

It's crucial to verify all visa and entry requirements closer to your travel date, as regulations can change. Always refer to official government sources or consult with the Czech embassy or consulate in your country for the most up-to-date and accurate information.

2.3 CURRENCY AND MONEY MATTERS IN THE CZECH REPUBLIC

Understanding the currency and money-related aspects is crucial for a seamless experience during your visit to the Czech Republic. Here's a detailed guide to help you navigate currency, banking, and financial considerations:

1. **Currency:**
    - The official currency of the Czech Republic is the Czech Crown (CZK), locally known as "Koruna."

- Notes come in denominations of 100, 200, 500, 1000, 2000, and 5000 CZK.
- Coins are available in denominations of 1, 2, 5, 10, 20, and 50 CZK.

2. Currency Exchange:
- Currency exchange services are widely available at airports, banks, exchange offices, and hotels.
- While hotels may offer this service, rates might be less favorable compared to dedicated exchange offices.

3. ATMs and Credit Cards:
- ATMs (Bankomat) are prevalent and accept major credit and debit cards.
- Inform your bank about your travel dates to avoid card issues due to international transactions.
- Credit cards are widely accepted in larger establishments, but it's advisable to have some cash for smaller businesses and local markets.

4. Banking Hours:
- Banks in the Czech Republic typically operate from Monday to Friday, with varying opening hours.
- Larger cities may have banks with extended hours, while smaller towns may have limited operating times.

5. Tipping Culture:
- Tipping is common in restaurants, and rounding up the bill is customary.
- For exceptional service, a tip of around 10% is appreciated.

6. Goods and Service Tax (VAT):
- The standard VAT rate in the Czech Republic is 21%.
- Most prices displayed include VAT, but always check if it's included or not, especially in restaurants.

7. Shopping and Bargaining:
- Major credit cards are accepted in shopping centers and tourist areas.

- Bargaining is not a common practice in Czech shops, but you can try in markets or smaller establishments.

8. Traveler's Checks:
- Traveler's checks are becoming less common, and it may be challenging to find places that accept them.
- Using ATMs for cash withdrawal is often more convenient.

9. Mobile Payments:
- Mobile payment options are increasingly available in larger cities and tourist areas.
- Check if your payment app is compatible with local systems.

10. Budgeting:
- The cost of living in the Czech Republic is generally lower than in Western European countries.
- Plan your budget considering accommodation, meals, transportation, and activities.

11. Emergency Funds:
- Keep a small amount of local currency for emergencies and places that may not accept cards.
- Ensure you have access to emergency funds, such as a credit card, in case of unexpected expenses.

12. Currency Conversion Apps:
- Use currency conversion apps to stay updated on exchange rates.
- This can help you make informed decisions when exchanging money.

13. Scams and Safety:
- Be cautious when using ATMs in tourist areas to avoid potential scams.
- Keep an eye on your belongings, especially in crowded places.

14. Language Barrier:
- While many people in tourist areas speak English, learn basic Czech phrases for

money-related transactions to enhance communication.

By being well-informed about the local currency, banking facilities, and spending norms, you can make the most of your financial transactions in the Czech Republic, ensuring a seamless and enjoyable travel experience.

2.4 LANGUAGE AND COMMUNICATION TIPS

Navigating the linguistic landscape is an integral part of any travel experience. In the Czech

Republic, understanding the language and communication norms enhances your interaction with locals and enriches your journey. Here's an extensive guide:

1. Official Language:
The official language of the Czech Republic is Czech (čeština), a West Slavic language.
While English is widely spoken in tourist areas and larger cities, especially among the younger population, learning a few basic Czech phrases is appreciated and can go a long way.

2. Basic Czech Phrases:
- Hello - Ahoj (ahoy)
- Good morning - Dobré ráno (DOH-breh RAH-noh)
- Good afternoon - Dobré odpoledne (DOH-breh OHD-poh-LEHD-neh)
- Good evening - Dobrý večer (DOH-bree VECH-er)
- Thank you - Děkuji (DYEH-koo-yih)
- Please - Prosím (PROH-seem)

- Excuse me - S dovolením (S DOH-vo-leh-neem)
- Yes - Ano (AH-no)
- No - Ne (neh)
- Goodbye - Na shledanou (NAH SHLEH-dah-noh)

3. English Proficiency:
- English is commonly spoken in tourist-centric areas, hotels, and restaurants.
- In smaller towns or rural areas, locals might have limited English proficiency, so having a basic grasp of Czech can be beneficial.

4. Politeness and Formality:
- The Czech language has formal and informal forms of addressing individuals.
- When in doubt, it's generally safe to use the formal address (vy) until invited to use the informal (ty).

5. Learning Czech:
- While not necessary, learning more complex phrases or using language learning apps can enhance your experience.
- Czechs often appreciate efforts to speak their language, even if it's basic.

6. Public Transportation Announcements:
- Public transportation announcements, including metro and tram stops, are usually made in both Czech and English in larger cities.

7. Tourist Information Centers:
- Tourist information centers are staffed with English-speaking personnel who can assist with maps, recommendations, and directions.

8. Technology and Translation Apps:
- Utilize translation apps for on-the-go assistance.

- Offline translation apps can be particularly useful, especially in areas with limited internet connectivity.

9. Cultural Sensitivity in Communication:
Czech people appreciate politeness and respect. When entering a room or joining a group, a general greeting is customary.

10. Signage:
- Public signs, especially in tourist areas, are often in both Czech and English.
- -In more remote areas, having a translation app can help decipher signs.

11. Dialects and Regional Variations:
- Be aware that dialects and regional variations exist.
- Some phrases may have different meanings in various parts of the country.

12. Emergency Phrases:
- Familiarize yourself with emergency phrases or numbers (such as calling for help) in Czech.
- Common emergency number: 112.

13. Czech Culture and Communication:
- Understanding cultural nuances is as important as language.
- Czechs may be reserved initially, but they appreciate direct and honest communication.

14. Local Media:
- Watching local television or listening to radio broadcasts in Czech can help familiarize you with the language and accent.

15. Enjoy the Learning Process:
- Embrace the opportunity to learn and engage with the local language.

- Locals often respond positively to visitors who make an effort to communicate in Czech.

By incorporating these language and communication tips, you can enhance your cultural experience and build meaningful connections during your time in the Czech Republic. Whether interacting with locals, navigating public spaces, or immersing yourself in the culture, a thoughtful approach to communication contributes to a more enriching travel experience.

3.0 DESTINATIONS

3.1 PRAGUE: A MAGNIFICENT CITY OF HISTORY AND CULTURE

Prague, often referred to as "the City of a Hundred Spires," is the capital and largest city of the Czech Republic. Nestled along the Vltava River, this enchanting city is a captivating blend of historical charm, architectural wonders, and a vibrant cultural scene. Here's an extensive overview of what makes Prague a must-visit destination:

1. Historical Heritage:
Prague boasts a rich history dating back over a thousand years. Its well-preserved Old Town, Prague Castle, and historical bridges reflect a tapestry of medieval, Gothic, Renaissance, and Baroque influences.

2. Prague Castle:
Dominating the city's skyline, Prague Castle is one of the largest ancient castles in the world. The complex includes St. Vitus Cathedral, Old Royal Palace, and Golden Lane, offering a journey through centuries of Czech history.

3. Charles Bridge:
This iconic bridge, adorned with statues of saints, spans the Vltava River, connecting the Old Town and Prague Castle. Charles Bridge is not just a crossing; it's a picturesque destination with stunning views of the city.

4. Old Town Square:
The heart of Prague's historic center, Old Town Square, is surrounded by colorful buildings, the

Astronomical Clock, and the imposing Church of Our Lady before Týn. It's a hub of activity with street performers, markets, and charming cafes.

5. Astronomical Clock (Orloj):

Installed in the Old Town Square in 1410, the Astronomical Clock is a medieval marvel. Every hour, crowds gather to witness the clock's animated figurines and the "Walk of the Apostles."

6. Josefov (Jewish Quarter):

Explore the Jewish Quarter, with its synagogues, the Jewish Cemetery, and the historic Old Jewish Town Hall. It's a testament to Prague's diverse and resilient Jewish heritage.

7. Wenceslas Square:

A vibrant boulevard lined with shops, hotels, and restaurants, Wenceslas Square is a modern contrast to the city's historical sites. It has been a central location for many significant events in Czech history.

8. Museums and Galleries:
Prague is home to numerous museums, including the National Museum, the Museum of Communism, and the Franz Kafka Museum. Art enthusiasts can explore the National Gallery and the Museum Kampa.

9. Cultural Events:
Prague hosts a myriad of cultural events throughout the year. The Prague Spring International Music Festival, Prague Fringe Festival, and various film festivals contribute to the city's vibrant cultural calendar.

10. Czech Cuisine:
Indulge in traditional Czech cuisine. Try classics like svíčková (marinated beef with creamy sauce), trdelník (a sweet pastry), and, of course, Czech beer, renowned for its quality and variety.

11. Vibrant Nightlife:
Prague comes alive at night with its diverse nightlife scene. From historic pubs and jazz

clubs to modern bars and nightclubs, there's something for everyone.

12. Petrin Hill and Prague Funicular:
For panoramic views of the city, climb Petrin Hill or take the funicular to the top. The Petrin Tower offers breathtaking vistas, and the hill is dotted with parks and gardens.

13. Bohemian Art and Craft:
Explore the bohemian art and craft scene in neighborhoods like Malá Strana. Discover unique boutiques, galleries, and studios showcasing local creativity.

14. River Cruises:
Enjoy a relaxing cruise along the Vltava River, offering a different perspective of Prague's skyline and landmarks.

Prague's enchanting ambiance, architectural marvels, and rich cultural tapestry make it a city that effortlessly blends the old and the new. Whether you're wandering through narrow cobblestone streets or marveling at Gothic cathedrals, Prague promises an unforgettable experience that transports you through centuries of history and cultural evolution.

3.1.1 Old Town Square: Prague's Historical Heart

Prague's Old Town Square, or Staroměstské náměstí, stands as a picturesque and vibrant centerpiece that encapsulates the city's rich history and architectural splendor. This medieval square, surrounded by stunning buildings and brimming with activity, is a must-visit destination for anyone exploring the Czech capital. Let's delve into the enchanting features that make Old Town Square a captivating historical and cultural hub:

1. Historical Significance:
Old Town Square dates back to the 12th century and has been the focal point of Prague's historical events and cultural life for centuries.

2. Astronomical Clock (Orloj):

One of the main attractions in the square is the Astronomical Clock on the Old Town Hall. Installed in 1410, it's the third-oldest astronomical clock in the world. Visitors gather hourly to witness its animated figurines and celestial display.

3. Old Town Hall Tower:

The Old Town Hall Tower offers panoramic views of Prague's rooftops and landmarks. Climbing to the top provides a breathtaking perspective of the city.

4. Church of Our Lady before Týn:

Dominating the skyline with its distinctive twin spires, this Gothic masterpiece is a key feature of the square. Its interior is equally impressive, housing Baroque altars and a stunning organ.

5. Jan Hus Memorial:

The memorial, dedicated to the Czech reformer Jan Hus, is a prominent statue in the square. It adds a touch of historical significance and represents Czech national pride.

6. St. Nicholas Church:
This Baroque church, with its impressive dome, is a prominent feature on the square. Its interior showcases lavish decoration and intricate frescoes.

7. Týn Cathedral:
The Church of Our Lady before Týn, commonly known as Týn Cathedral, is a striking Gothic structure with a dark and imposing facade. Its interior holds notable works of art.

8. Old Town Square Christmas Market:
During the festive season, Old Town Square transforms into a winter wonderland with its Christmas market. Visitors can enjoy mulled wine, traditional Czech treats, and handmade crafts.

9. Street Performers and Artists:
The square is often filled with street performers, musicians, and artists, creating a lively atmosphere. This adds a contemporary touch to the historical surroundings.

10. Historical Houses:
The square is surrounded by elegant historical houses with colorful facades, each telling a story of Prague's past. The House at the Minute and the Stone Bell House are notable examples.

11. Restaurants and Cafés:
The square is lined with charming restaurants and cafés where you can savor Czech cuisine or enjoy a coffee while soaking in the surroundings.

12. Cultural Events:
Old Town Square hosts various cultural events and festivals throughout the year, from concerts to outdoor performances. It's a dynamic space that embraces both tradition and modernity.

13. Easter Markets:
In spring, the square comes alive with vibrant Easter markets featuring traditional crafts, festive decorations, and seasonal treats.

14. New Year's Eve Celebrations:
Old Town Square is a popular spot for ringing in the New Year. The square hosts a festive celebration with fireworks and a lively atmosphcrc.

Old Town Square is a captivating blend of architectural beauty, cultural richness, and a lively atmosphere. Whether you're admiring centuries-old structures or enjoying the dynamic energy of contemporary events, this historic square offers a captivating journey through Prague's past and present.

3.1.2 Prague Castle: A Majestic Symbol of Czech History and Culture

Perched high above the Vltava River, Prague Castle stands as a majestic testament to the rich history and cultural heritage of the Czech Republic. This sprawling complex, often cited as the largest ancient castle in the world, is a must-visit destination for those seeking to explore the heart of Prague's historical and architectural wonders. Let's delve into the enchanting features that make Prague Castle a captivating symbol of Czech history:

1. Historical Origins:

Prague Castle's origins trace back to the 9th century when it was founded by Prince Bořivoj of the Premyslid Dynasty. Over the centuries, it evolved into a complex amalgamation of various architectural styles.

2. Architectural Marvels:

The castle complex showcases a diverse range of architectural styles, including Gothic, Romanesque, Baroque, and Renaissance. Notable structures include St. Vitus Cathedral, Old Royal Palace, and the Basilica of St. George.

3. St. Vitus Cathedral:

The crown jewel of Prague Castle, St. Vitus Cathedral, is a masterpiece of Gothic architecture. Its soaring spires and intricate stained glass windows make it a stunning symbol of Czech religious and cultural identity.

4. Old Royal Palace:

This historic palace served as the seat of Czech kings, emperors, and presidents. The Vladislav Hall within the palace witnessed significant events, including royal banquets and coronations.

5. Golden Lane:

Nestled within the castle grounds, Golden Lane is a charming street of colorful houses that once housed castle defenders. Today, it offers a glimpse into medieval life with its small shops and exhibits.

6. Basilica of St. George:

Dating back to the 10th century, the Basilica of St. George is one of the oldest surviving churches in Prague. Its Romanesque architecture and historical artifacts provide a window into early Czech Christianity.

7. Royal Gardens:
The expansive gardens surrounding Prague Castle offer a serene escape from the bustling city. Visitors can stroll through well-manicured lawns, admire statues, and enjoy panoramic views of the city below.

8. Changing of the Guard:
Experience the ceremonial Changing of the Guard at Prague Castle, a daily spectacle that takes place at the entrance gates. The guards' colorful uniforms and precise choreography add a touch of tradition to the visit.

9. Dalibor Tower:
- Dalibor Tower, a cylindrical structure with a dark past, is part of the castle complex. It served as a prison, and its eerie atmosphere provides a glimpse into medieval justice.

10. Summer Shakespeare Performances:
The castle courtyard comes alive during the summer months with open-air performances of Shakespearean plays. The unique setting adds a

touch of theatrical magic to the historic surroundings.

11. Prague Castle Picture Gallery:
- Art enthusiasts can explore the Prague Castle Picture Gallery, home to an impressive collection of European paintings, including works by renowned artists such as Titian and Rubens.

12. Presidential Residence:
Today, Prague Castle serves as the official residence of the President of the Czech Republic. While some areas are reserved for official functions, much of the complex is open to the public.

13. Panoramic Views:
The elevated location of Prague Castle provides panoramic views of the city below. Sunset visits offer a particularly breathtaking backdrop of the Vltava River and Prague's skyline.

14. Cultural Events:

Prague Castle hosts a variety of cultural events, including classical concerts, art exhibitions, and historical reenactments. These events contribute to the castle's dynamic role as a cultural hub.

Prague Castle is not merely a historical monument; it's a living testament to the resilience and cultural richness of the Czech people. Its architectural splendor, historical significance, and vibrant atmosphere make it a must-visit destination for those eager to immerse themselves in the captivating story of Prague and the Czech Republic.

3.1.3 Charles Bridge: A Timeless Icon Connecting Prague's History

Charles Bridge, or Karlův most in Czech, is an iconic structure that gracefully spans the Vltava River, connecting the Old Town and Lesser Town (Malá Strana) of Prague. This historic bridge, steeped in legend and adorned with statuary, is not just a picturesque crossing; it's a symbol of Prague's rich history and architectural splendor. Let's explore the enchanting features that make Charles Bridge an integral part of Prague's cultural tapestry:

1. Historical Roots:
Construction of Charles Bridge began in 1357 under the reign of Charles IV, after the previous Judith Bridge was damaged by floods. The bridge took its current name from the monarch who commissioned its construction.

2. Architectural Beauty:
Charles Bridge is a stunning example of Gothic architecture, featuring 16 arches and three bridge towers. The bridge's sandstone blocks give it a warm, golden hue, especially during sunrise and sunset.

3. Statues and Sculptures:
The bridge is adorned with a series of 30 statues and statuaries, many of which are replicas (the originals were moved to the National Museum to preserve them). Notable sculptures include the statue of St. John of Nepomuk and the Crucifixion.

4. St. John of Nepomuk Statue:
The statue of St. John of Nepomuk is one of the most recognized and revered on the bridge. Touching the bronze relief of the priest is believed to bring good luck and ensure your return to Prague.

5. Old Town Bridge Tower:
The Old Town Bridge Tower on the eastern end of the bridge serves as a dramatic entrance to the Old Town. Climbing to the top provides panoramic views of Prague and the castle.

6. Lesser Town Bridge Tower:
The Lesser Town Bridge Tower on the western end offers equally stunning views and serves as a gateway to Lesser Town. Both towers were designed to make the bridge look like a triumphal arch.

7. Legends and Lore:
Charles Bridge is steeped in legends, including one about the egg yolks mixed into the mortar for added strength and another about Master

Hanuš, the supposed architect who was later blinded to prevent him from replicating such beauty.

8. Easter Markets:
During the Easter season, Charles Bridge hosts festive markets with stalls offering traditional crafts, Easter decorations, and seasonal treats. It's a delightful way to experience local traditions.

9. Street Performers and Artists:
- The bridge is a lively hub with street performers, musicians, and artists. Visitors can enjoy live music, portrait sketches, and the vibrant atmosphere created by artists showcasing their talents.

10. Vltava River Views:
Walking along Charles Bridge provides breathtaking views of the Vltava River and the surrounding cityscape. Photographers often capture the bridge's silhouette against the backdrop of Prague Castle.

11. Historic Crossings:
Charles Bridge was the only river crossing in Prague until 1841. Its importance as a trade route contributed to the city's growth and prosperity.

12. Sunset Strolls:
Sunset is a magical time on Charles Bridge. As the sun sets over the Vltava, the bridge's sculptures and towers are bathed in warm, golden light, creating a truly enchanting ambiance.

13. New Year's Eve Fireworks:
Charles Bridge is a popular spot for watching New Year's Eve fireworks, offering a front-row seat to the spectacular displays over the Vltava River.

14. Locks of Love:
Visitors often attach love locks to the bridge's railings as a symbol of enduring love. While this tradition is now discouraged due to preservation

concerns, remnants of the practice can still be seen.

Charles Bridge isn't just a physical link between two parts of Prague; it's a bridge through time, connecting the city's past with its vibrant present. Its architectural grace, historical significance, and the lively spirit that envelops it make Charles Bridge a must-visit destination for those seeking to immerse themselves in the timeless allure of Prague.

3.2 ČESKÝ KRUMLOV: A FAIRYTALE TOWN ALONG THE VLTAVA RIVER

Nestled in the heart of Southern Bohemia, Český Krumlov is a charming town that seems to have stepped out of a fairytale. Its well-preserved medieval architecture, meandering cobblestone streets, and the meandering Vltava River contribute to a magical atmosphere that transports visitors to another era. Let's explore the enchanting features that make Český Krumlov a must-visit destination:

1. UNESCO World Heritage Site:
Český Krumlov's historical center, with its medieval layout and architecture, is recognized as a UNESCO World Heritage Site. The town's preservation efforts have maintained its unique charm.

2. Český Krumlov Castle:
Dominating the town's skyline, Český Krumlov Castle is a sprawling complex that evolved over centuries. Visitors can explore the castle's courtyards, gardens, and interiors, including the Baroque Theatre.

3. Baroque Theatre:
The Baroque Theatre within the castle is one of the best-preserved of its kind in the world. The ornate stage machinery and original costumes provide a glimpse into historical theatrical performances.

4. Castle Gardens:
The terraced Castle Gardens offer panoramic views of Český Krumlov and the Vltava River. The manicured lawns, sculptures, and fountains make it a tranquil escape.

5. Vltava River:
The Vltava River winds its way around Český Krumlov, adding to the town's picturesque setting. Visitors can take leisurely walks along the riverbanks or enjoy boat rides for a unique perspective.

6. Český Krumlov State Castle Theatre:
This unique theater, located within the castle complex, is a functioning Baroque theater with original stage machinery. Summer performances transport audiences to the past with period-appropriate plays.

7. St. Vitus Church:
St. Vitus Church, located in the town square, is a Gothic masterpiece with a beautifully adorned

interior. Climb the church tower for panoramic views of Český Krumlov.

8. Historical Town Square:
The town square, surrounded by colorful Renaissance and Baroque buildings, is a hub of activity. Cafés, shops, and galleries line the square, creating a lively atmosphere.

9. Český Krumlov Castle Tower:
Climbing the castle tower offers stunning vistas of the town and its surroundings. It's a great vantage point for capturing the town's rooftops and the meandering river.

10. Egon Schiele Art Centrum:
Dedicated to the Austrian painter Egon Schiele, this center features exhibitions and workshops. It adds a contemporary touch to the town's cultural scene.

11. Museum of Torture Instruments:

For those intrigued by history's darker side, the Museum of Torture Instruments provides a chilling look at medieval punishment methods.

12. Craftsmen's Lane:
Craftsmen's Lane, nestled within the castle complex, is a narrow alley lined with small artisan workshops. Visitors can watch craftsmen at work and purchase handmade souvenirs.

13. Český Krumlov International Music Festival:
The town hosts an annual music festival, attracting renowned musicians and performers. The festival's venues, including the castle courtyard, contribute to its unique charm.

14. Festivals and Events:
Throughout the year, Český Krumlov hosts various events, including historical reenactments, folklore festivals, and Christmas markets.

15. Cultural Heritage:
Český Krumlov's commitment to preserving its cultural heritage is evident in its well-maintained architecture, historical sites, and efforts to showcase traditional crafts and arts.

Český Krumlov's timeless beauty, cultural richness, and the blend of history and artistic vibrancy make it a destination that captivates the imagination. Whether strolling along cobblestone streets, exploring the castle complex, or enjoying the riverside ambiance, visitors find themselves immersed in the enchanting allure of this fairytale town.

3.3 KARLOVY VARY: A SPA TOWN OF ELEGANCE AND WELLNESS

Nestled in the picturesque valleys of Western Bohemia, Karlovy Vary, also known as Carlsbad, is a renowned spa town celebrated for its elegant architecture, healing thermal springs, and a rich cultural history. This charming destination has attracted visitors seeking relaxation and rejuvenation for centuries. Let's explore the enchanting features that make Karlovy Vary a unique and therapeutic retreat:

1. Thermal Springs:
Karlovy Vary is famous for its thermal mineral springs, each believed to have distinct healing properties. The hot springs, with temperatures ranging from 30 to 72 degrees Celsius, form the basis of the town's spa culture.

2. Colonnades:
The town is adorned with impressive colonnades that shelter the thermal springs. Notable colonnades include the Mill Colonnade, Market Colonnade, and Park Colonnade, where visitors can sample the mineral waters directly from the springs.

3. Mill Colonnade:
The Mill Colonnade is a stunning architectural gem, housing several hot springs. Its elaborate design and decorative elements make it a focal point for both relaxation and architectural appreciation.

4. Spa Treatments:
Karlovy Vary offers a plethora of spa treatments, ranging from traditional mineral baths to modern wellness therapies. Visitors can indulge in therapeutic massages, mud wraps, and other wellness experiences.

5. Diana Observation Tower:
For panoramic views of the town and the surrounding landscape, visitors can ascend the Diana Observation Tower. It provides a breathtaking perspective of Karlovy Vary and the lush forests that surround it.

6. Grandhotel Pupp:
The Grandhotel Pupp, an opulent establishment with a rich history, has hosted prominent guests,

including celebrities and dignitaries. Its grandeur and elegance contribute to the town's allure.

7. Karlový Vary International Film Festival:

The town hosts one of the oldest and most prestigious film festivals in the world. The Karlovy Vary International Film Festival attracts filmmakers, actors, and cinema enthusiasts, adding a cultural vibrancy to the town.

8. Moser Glass Museum:

Renowned for its glassmaking heritage, Karlovy Vary is home to the Moser Glass Museum. The museum showcases exquisite glassware, crystal creations, and the history of glassmaking in the region.

9. Vřídlo Spring:

Vřídlo, the hottest spring in Karlovy Vary, shoots water up to 12 meters high. The Vřídlo Colonnade provides a dramatic setting to witness this natural spectacle.

10. Czech Traditional Liqueur:
Be sure to sample the local herbal liqueur, Becherovka, renowned for its unique blend of spices and herbs. It's often enjoyed as a digestive after spa treatments.

11. Teplá Monastery:
Explore the Teplá Monastery, a historic complex with a Baroque-style church and a library housing valuable manuscripts. The monastery's tranquil surroundings offer a peaceful retreat.

12. Karlovy Vary Museum:
The Karlovy Vary Museum delves into the town's history, spa traditions, and showcases artifacts related to famous visitors. It provides insights into the cultural evolution of the region.

13. Karlsbad Porcelain:
Karlovy Vary is known for its fine porcelain. Visitors can purchase exquisite porcelain items as souvenirs, adding a touch of elegance to their homes.

14. Hiking Trails:
Surrounding the town are scenic hiking trails that lead to viewpoints, nature reserves, and hidden gems in the picturesque landscape.

Karlovy Vary's combination of natural beauty, spa culture, and cultural events makes it a destination that appeals to those seeking relaxation, cultural exploration, and the therapeutic benefits of mineral springs. Whether immersing oneself in spa treatments, exploring historic landmarks, or simply enjoying the elegant atmosphere, Karlovy Vary offers a rejuvenating and enriching experience.

3.4 BRNO: THE DYNAMIC HEART OF MORAVIA

Brno, the second-largest city in the Czech Republic, is a vibrant and culturally rich destination situated in the heart of Moravia. Known for its blend of historic charm and modern dynamism, Brno offers visitors a diverse range of experiences, from exploring centuries-old architecture to embracing the city's lively cultural scene. Let's delve into the features that make Brno a captivating destination:

1. Špilberk Castle:

Špilberk Castle, perched on a hill overlooking the city, is a symbol of Brno's history. Originally a fortress, it evolved into a royal castle and later served as a prison. Today, it houses a museum and offers panoramic views of Brno.

2. Cathedral of St. Peter and Paul:

This impressive Gothic cathedral dominates the city skyline. Its twin towers and intricate architecture make it a significant landmark. Visitors can climb to the top for stunning views of Brno.

3. Freedom Square (Náměstí Svobody):

The central square is a hub of activity, surrounded by historical buildings, shops, and cafés. It hosts events, markets, and is a gathering place for both locals and tourists.

4. Astronomical Clock:
Brno boasts its own Astronomical Clock, located on the Old Town Hall. While not as famous as Prague's clock, it's a charming piece of history and craftsmanship.

5. Vila Tugendhat:
A UNESCO World Heritage Site, Vila Tugendhat is a modernist architectural gem designed by Ludwig Mies van der Rohe. Guided tours offer insight into its innovative design and historical significance.

6. Brno Reservoir (Brněnská přehrada):
A popular recreational area, the Brno Reservoir offers opportunities for water sports, hiking, and relaxation. It's a great escape from the urban hustle.

7. Labyrinth Under Vegetable Market:
Beneath the Vegetable Market lies a labyrinth of historic cellars. Guided tours reveal Brno's medieval past, including stories of alchemy and espionage.

8. Moravian Gallery in Brno:
Art enthusiasts can explore the Moravian Gallery, housing an extensive collection of Czech and international art. The collection spans various periods, from Gothic to contemporary.

9. Mendel Museum:
Brno is the hometown of Gregor Mendel, the father of modern genetics. The Mendel Museum, located at the Augustinian Abbey where Mendel conducted his experiments, showcases his scientific contributions.

10. Lužánky Park:
Lužánky Park, the oldest public park in Central Europe, provides a green oasis in the city. It's a popular spot for leisurely walks, picnics, and outdoor activities.

11. Brno Underground:
Explore the extensive network of underground passages and cellars beneath the city. The Brno

Underground tour unveils hidden spaces with historical and architectural significance.

12. Veveri Castle:
Located on the shores of the Brno Reservoir, Veveri Castle is a picturesque fortress with a rich history. It's accessible by boat or hiking trails, offering a scenic excursion.

13. Brno Circuit:
Motorsport enthusiasts can visit the Masaryk Circuit, known for hosting MotoGP and other racing events. The circuit's museum showcases the history of motorsport in Brno.

14. Cultural Events:
Brno hosts a variety of cultural events, including music festivals, theater performances, and art exhibitions. The city's cultural calendar is dynamic, catering to diverse tastes.

15. Local Cuisine:
Indulge in Moravian cuisine, known for its hearty dishes and delicious wines. Try traditional

specialties like svíčková (marinated beef), bramborák (potato pancake), and Moravian wine.

Brno's dynamic character, historical landmarks, and cultural offerings make it a destination that appeals to a broad range of interests. Whether exploring medieval castles, enjoying modernist architecture, or partaking in the city's lively cultural events, Brno invites visitors to discover the unique blend of its rich heritage and contemporary vitality.

3.5 PLZEŇ: WHERE BEER, HISTORY, AND CULTURE CONVERGE

Plzeň, also known as Pilsen in German, is a city with a rich brewing heritage, historical significance, and a vibrant cultural scene. Located in western Bohemia, Plzeň has become synonymous with the birthplace of Pilsner beer. Let's explore the unique features that make Plzeň a captivating destination:

1. Pilsner Urquell Brewery:

Plzeň is the birthplace of the world-famous Pilsner beer. Visitors can tour the Pilsner Urquell Brewery to learn about the brewing process, explore historical cellars, and enjoy a freshly tapped Pilsner straight from the source.

2. Pilsen Historic Underground:
Delve into the city's history by exploring the Pilsen Historic Underground. Guided tours take visitors through medieval cellars, revealing secrets of the past, including brewing practices and trade routes.

3. St. Bartholomew's Cathedral:
The towering St. Bartholomew's Cathedral dominates the cityscape. Its Gothic architecture and impressive interior, including the highest church spire in the Czech Republic, make it a must-visit landmark.

4. Pilsen Town Hall:
The Pilsen Town Hall, situated in the main square, is a striking Renaissance building.

Visitors can climb to the top for panoramic views of the city.

5. Techmania Science Center:
Ideal for families and science enthusiasts, the Techmania Science Center offers interactive exhibits and experiments covering various scientific disciplines.

6. Great Synagogue:
The Great Synagogue, one of the largest synagogues in Europe, is an architectural gem. Its Moorish Revival style and rich history make it a significant cultural site.

7. Patton Memorial Pilsen:
Pilsen played a crucial role in World War II, and the Patton Memorial honors General George S. Patton, whose troops liberated the city. The memorial is located near the Pilsner Urquell Brewery.

8. Pilsen Zoo:

The Pilsen Zoo is a popular attraction with a diverse range of animals and educational programs. It provides a delightful experience for visitors of all ages.

9. Pilsen Puppet Museum:
Puppetry has a rich tradition in the Czech Republic, and the Pilsen Puppet Museum showcases the art and history of puppetry through a fascinating collection.

10. Museum of West Bohemia in Pilsen:
Explore the Museum of West Bohemia, which houses extensive exhibits on regional history, art, and culture. The museum's collections include artifacts from various periods.

11. Pilsen City Park:
The City Park, with its scenic landscapes and walking paths, offers a peaceful retreat. It's an ideal spot for leisurely strolls and relaxation.

12. Brewery Restaurants:
Beyond the Pilsner Urquell Brewery, Plzeň boasts a variety of brewery restaurants where visitors can sample local beers and traditional Czech dishes.

13. Pilsen Film Festival:
Film enthusiasts can attend the Pilsen Film Festival, which celebrates Czech and international cinema. The festival screens a diverse selection of films and hosts discussions and events.

14. Street Art Scene:
Plzeň has a burgeoning street art scene, with colorful murals and installations adding a contemporary flair to the city's streets.

15. Local Cuisine:
Indulge in Czech cuisine at local restaurants, where hearty dishes like svíčková (marinated beef), knedlíky (dumplings), and, of course, traditional Pilsner beer are on the menu.

Plzeň's unique blend of brewing tradition, historical landmarks, and cultural offerings makes it a destination that caters to a diverse range of interests. Whether exploring the brewing heritage, discovering hidden underground passages, or immersing oneself in the city's vibrant cultural scene, Plzeň invites visitors to savor the essence of Czech history and hospitality.

3.6 KUTNÁ HORA: A MEDIEVAL GEM WITH GOTHIC SPLENDOR

Kutná Hora, a town with medieval charm nestled in the heart of Bohemia, is renowned for its historical significance and stunning Gothic architecture. Once a prosperous silver mining center, Kutná Hora has preserved its rich heritage, attracting visitors with its unique sites. Let's explore the enchanting features that make Kutná Hora a captivating destination:

1. St. Barbara's Cathedral:
St. Barbara's Cathedral, a UNESCO World Heritage Site, is a masterpiece of Gothic architecture. Its intricate details, soaring spires, and stunning interior make it one of the most impressive cathedrals in the Czech Republic.

2. Sedlec Ossuary (Kostnice):
The Sedlec Ossuary, also known as the Bone Church, is a fascinating and somewhat macabre site. Decorated with human bones, the ossuary is both eerie and artistically intriguing.

3. Historic City Center:
The historic city center of Kutná Hora is a labyrinth of narrow cobblestone streets, charming squares, and well-preserved medieval buildings. The architecture reflects the town's prosperous past.

4. Italian Court (Vlašský dvůr):
The Italian Court, a royal residence and mint, showcases Renaissance architecture. Visitors can

explore its medieval halls and the Minting House, where silver coins were once produced.

5. Czech Museum of Silver (České muzeum stříbra):

Learn about the town's silver mining history at the Czech Museum of Silver. The exhibits cover the economic, technological, and cultural aspects of Kutná Hora's mining heritage.

6. Barbora's House:

Barbora's House, named after St. Barbara, houses a permanent exhibition on medieval mining technology. The building itself is an example of Gothic and Renaissance architecture.

7. Royal Mint (Králův dům):

The Royal Mint, part of the Italian Court, is where the first Prague groschen was minted. Explore the coin-making process and the history of currency.

8. Stone Fountain (Kamenná kašna):

The Stone Fountain in the central square is a Renaissance masterpiece featuring sculptures and reliefs. It served as a source of drinking water for the townspeople.

9. Jesuit College:

The Jesuit College, an imposing Baroque building, houses the Kutná Hora Gallery of Fine Arts. It features a collection of European art from the 14th to 18th centuries.

10. Silver Mine Tours:

Take a guided tour of the Hrádek Museum, an old silver mine, to experience the conditions miners faced and gain insights into the town's mining history.

11. Hradek:
Hradek is a medieval fortress that once protected the mint and stored valuable documents. The fortress offers panoramic views of Kutná Hora and its surroundings.

12. Gallery of Modern Art (GASK):
The Gallery of Modern Art, housed in the Jesuit College, features contemporary Czech art. It adds a modern touch to Kutná Hora's cultural scene.

13. Festival of Silver:
The town hosts the Festival of Silver, celebrating its mining heritage with cultural events, music, and exhibitions. It's a vibrant time to experience Kutná Hora's cultural offerings.

14. Bohemiae Rosa Restaurant:
Enjoy traditional Czech cuisine in the medieval setting of Bohemiae Rosa Restaurant, located in the historic city center.

15. Czech Gothic Style:

Kutná Hora is a prime example of Czech Gothic architecture, with its churches, burgher houses, and fortifications showcasing the artistry and craftsmanship of the Gothic period.

Kutná Hora's blend of Gothic splendor, historical significance, and cultural attractions provides visitors with a captivating journey through medieval Bohemia. Whether exploring the intricacies of St. Barbara's Cathedral, contemplating the unique artistry of the Sedlec Ossuary, or wandering through the well-preserved city center, Kutná Hora invites travelers to step back in time and immerse themselves in its storied past.

3.7 OLOMOUC: A HIDDEN GEM OF BAROQUE BEAUTY

Olomouc, tucked away in the heart of Moravia, is a city steeped in history, adorned with Baroque architecture, and adorned with cultural treasures. Often overshadowed by larger Czech cities, Olomouc offers visitors a more intimate and authentic experience. Let's explore the enchanting features that make Olomouc a hidden gem:

1. Holy Trinity Column:

The Holy Trinity Column, a UNESCO World Heritage Site, is a Baroque masterpiece dominating the city's main square. Adorned with sculptures and intricate details, it symbolizes Olomouc's triumph over the plague.

2. Olomouc Astronomical Clock:

The Olomouc Astronomical Clock, situated on the Town Hall, is a marvel of medieval engineering. It features animated figurines and astronomical dials, captivating visitors with its hourly show.

3. St. Wenceslas Cathedral:

St. Wenceslas Cathedral, the principal church of Olomouc, boasts a mix of architectural styles, including Romanesque and Gothic. The views from its tower offer a panoramic look at the city.

4. Archbishop's Palace:

The Archbishop's Palace, a grand Baroque residence, is home to the Archdiocesan Museum.

Visitors can explore exhibits showcasing religious art and artifacts.

5. Olomouc Castle:
Olomouc Castle, with its historic halls and gardens, provides a serene escape. The castle complex includes the Archbishop's Palace and offers insights into Olomouc's ecclesiastical history.

6. Six Baroque Fountains:
Olomouc is renowned for its six Baroque fountains, each depicting mythological figures. The Caesar Fountain and Jupiter Fountain are among the most notable.

7. Horní náměstí (Upper Square):
The Upper Square is a picturesque space surrounded by colorful Baroque buildings, including the Town Hall and the Holy Trinity Column. It's a charming spot for leisurely strolls.

8. Lower Square (Dolní náměstí):
The Lower Square is another historic space, featuring the impressive Marian Column and the Church of St. Maurice.

9. Column of St. Florian:
The Column of St. Florian, located in the Lower Square, is a Baroque monument honoring the patron saint of firefighters.

10. Olomouc Botanical Gardens:
The Olomouc Botanical Gardens, founded in the 16th century, are among the oldest in Europe. They showcase a diverse collection of plants and provide a tranquil environment.

11. Cyclist Statue:
The Cyclist Statue, a quirky and beloved landmark, pays homage to the city's cycling culture. It adds a touch of whimsy to the streets of Olomouc.

12. Comenius University:
Comenius University, named after the educator John Amos Comenius, is a historic institution with a rich academic tradition.

13. Smetana Gardens:
Smetana Gardens, a green oasis in the city center, offer a peaceful retreat. The gardens feature sculptures, flower beds, and a delightful atmosphere.

14. Olomouc Cheese:
Don't miss the chance to taste Olomouc cheese, a pungent, soft cheese that has become a local delicacy. It's often served with bread or included in traditional dishes.

15. Cultural Events:
Olomouc hosts various cultural events throughout the year, including music festivals, art exhibitions, and historical reenactments. Check the local calendar for events during your visit.

Olomouc, with its rich cultural heritage, architectural splendor, and relaxed atmosphere, invites visitors to explore its hidden treasures. Whether wandering through historic squares, admiring Baroque masterpieces, or savoring local delicacies, Olomouc offers a unique and authentic Czech experience.

4.0 TRANSPORTATION

4.1 GETTING TO THE CZECH REPUBLIC: YOUR GATEWAY TO CENTRAL EUROPE

Traveling to the Czech Republic is a seamless experience, thanks to its well-connected transportation network and strategic location in the heart of Europe. Whether you're arriving by air, train, bus, or car, the Czech Republic offers various options to suit different preferences and travel styles.

BY AIR:

1. Václav Havel Airport Prague (PRG):
The main gateway to the Czech Republic by air is Václav Havel Airport Prague, located approximately 17 kilometers west of the city center. As the largest international airport in the country, it serves as a major hub for both European and intercontinental flights.

2. Regional Airports:

In addition to Prague, the Czech Republic has several regional airports, such as Brno-Tuřany Airport, Ostrava Leos Janacek Airport, and Karlovy Vary International Airport, providing convenient access to different parts of the country.

3. Airport Transportation:

From Václav Havel Airport Prague, travelers can easily reach the city center by taxi, private transfer, or public transport. The Airport Express bus offers a direct connection to Prague's main train station.

BY TRAIN:

1. International Rail Connections:
The Czech Republic is well-connected to neighboring European countries by an extensive rail network. International trains from cities like Vienna, Berlin, Munich, and Budapest offer comfortable and scenic journeys.

2. Prague Main Train Station (Praha hlavní nádraží):

Prague's main train station is a central transportation hub with excellent connections to domestic and international destinations. High-speed trains, such as EuroCity and Railjet, provide efficient travel to and from major European cities.

BY BUS:

1. International Bus Services:

Intercity and international bus services connect the Czech Republic to neighboring countries. Companies like FlixBus and Eurolines operate routes to and from major European cities.

2. Central Bus Stations:

Major cities, including Prague, Brno, and Ostrava, have central bus stations offering domestic and international services. These stations are often conveniently located in or near city centers.

BY CAR:

1. Road Networks

The Czech Republic has a well-maintained road infrastructure, making it accessible by car. European highways, such as the E55 and E65, connect the country to neighboring states.

2. Border Crossings

Numerous border crossings facilitate entry into the Czech Republic by road. Travelers should be aware of the specific requirements and regulations when crossing international borders.

VISA REQUIREMENTS
1. Schengen Area:

The Czech Republic is part of the Schengen Area, allowing travelers from Schengen countries to move freely across borders without passport control. However, visitors from non-Schengen countries may need a visa.

2. Schengen Visa

Travelers requiring a visa must apply for a Schengen Visa at the Czech embassy or consulate in their home country. It's essential to check visa requirements well in advance of travel.

COMMUNITY SHUTTLES
1. Public Transport:
Within cities and towns, efficient public transportation systems, including buses, trams, and metro services, make it easy to navigate and explore local attractions.

2. Taxis and Ride-Sharing:
Taxis are readily available in urban areas, and ride-sharing services operate in major cities. It's advisable to use licensed services and agree on fares in advance.

TRAVEL TIPS:
1. Currency:
The official currency is the Czech koruna (CZK). ATMs are widely available, and credit cards are accepted in most establishments.

2. Language:
The official language is Czech, but English is commonly spoken in tourist areas and major cities.

3. Weather Considerations:
The climate varies, so it's essential to pack accordingly. Winters can be cold, while summers are generally mild to warm.

4. Cultural Etiquette:
Respecting local customs and etiquette enhances the travel experience. Greetings, tipping practices, and table manners may differ from those in other countries.

Whether arriving by air, train, bus, or car, getting to the Czech Republic sets the stage for a journey into the heart of Central Europe. With its rich history, stunning landscapes, and vibrant cities, the Czech Republic welcomes travelers to explore its diverse attractions and immerse themselves in the charm of this captivating destination.

4.2 LOCAL TRANSPORTATION

The Czech Republic boasts a well-developed and efficient transportation system, making it convenient for residents and visitors to explore both urban centers and the picturesque countryside. From public transport in cities to long-distance travel options, here's an extensive overview of local transportation in the Czech Republic:

URBAN PUBLIC TRANSPORTATION
1. Trams
Cities Served: Trams are a common mode of transport in major cities such as Prague, Brno, and Ostrava.

Features: Extensive tram networks cover key areas, providing a reliable and environmentally friendly way to move around. Trams are known for their frequency and coverage of urban districts.

2. Buses
Cities Served: Buses operate in cities and towns across the country, connecting neighborhoods and suburbs.

Features: Bus routes complement tram networks, offering flexibility and accessibility to areas not covered by trams. Inter-city buses provide connections to neighboring regions.

3. Metro
Cities Served: Prague is the only city in the Czech Republic with a metro system.
Features: The Prague Metro consists of three lines, providing rapid transit within the city. It's a quick and efficient way to navigate Prague, especially for longer distances.

4. Trolleybuses
Cities Served: Trolleybuses operate in cities like Brno and Plzeň.
Features: Trolleybuses, powered by overhead wires, offer a clean and quiet mode of transport. They contribute to sustainable urban mobility and are part of the public transportation network.

INTER-CITY TRANSPORTATION
1. Trains
Rail Network: The Czech Republic has an extensive and well-maintained rail network.
Services: Inter-city trains connect major cities, offering a comfortable and scenic way to travel between regions. High-speed and international

trains provide efficient links to neighboring countries.

2. Buses

Long-Distance Services: Long-distance buses operate between cities and towns, providing an alternative to trains.

Flexibility: Buses are a flexible option for reaching destinations not directly served by trains. Companies like FlixBus offer convenient connections to various European cities.

INTERCITY ROAD TRAVEL
1. Cars

Road Network: The Czech Republic has well-maintained roads and highways.

Car Rentals: Renting a car is a popular choice for exploring rural areas and scenic landscapes. It offers flexibility and the opportunity to visit off-the-beaten-path destinations.

2. Ride-Sharing

Services: Ride-sharing services like Uber operate in major cities, providing an on-demand and convenient option for local travel.

TRAVEL TIPS
1. Integrated Ticketing

Cities: Many cities offer integrated ticketing systems, allowing passengers to use a single ticket for trams, buses, and metro services within a specified time frame.

2. Czech Rail Pass

Benefits: Travelers planning to explore multiple cities by train can consider the Czech Rail Pass. It offers flexibility and cost savings for unlimited travel within a set period.

3. Transportation Apps

Useful Apps: Apps like IDOS (Integrated Transport System) and public transport apps in major cities provide real-time information on routes, schedules, and ticket prices.

4. Bike Rentals
Biking: Many cities, especially Prague, offer bike-sharing programs and bike rentals, providing an eco-friendly way to explore urban areas.

5. Prague Card
Features: Visitors to Prague can benefit from the Prague Card, which includes unlimited use of public transportation, including trams, buses, and the metro, within the city.

ACCESSIBILITY
1. Disability-Friendly Services
Initiatives: Efforts have been made to improve accessibility in public transport for people with disabilities. Many trams and buses are equipped with ramps, and metro stations have elevators.

2. Information in English
English Language: Most transportation information, including signage and ticket

machines, is available in English, making it accessible to international travelers.

From the bustling streets of Prague to the tranquil countryside, the Czech Republic's local transportation options cater to a variety of travel preferences. Whether you prefer the convenience of public transport in cities, the flexibility of long-distance buses, or the freedom of exploring by car, the country's transportation infrastructure ensures that every corner is within reach for those eager to discover its beauty and charm.

4.3 RENTING A CAR IN THE CZECH REPUBLIC: FREEDOM TO EXPLORE THE HEART OF EUROPE

Renting a car in the Czech Republic is a fantastic way to unlock the country's full potential, offering the freedom to explore medieval towns, picturesque landscapes, and historic landmarks at your own pace. Here's an extensive guide to help you navigate the process of renting a car and experiencing the beauty of the Czech Republic:

CAR RENTAL COMPANIES

1. International Brands
Renowned international car rental companies such as Hertz, Avis, Budget, and Europcar operate in major cities and airports, providing a wide range of vehicle options.

2. Local Agencies
Local car rental agencies, like Czech Car Hire and Rent Plus, also offer competitive services, often providing a personal touch and additional flexibility.

REQUIREMENTS FOR RENTING A CAR

1. Driving License

A valid driving license is essential. International visitors from non-EU countries may need an International Driving Permit (IDP), which is a translation of their home country's license.

2. Age Restrictions

Most car rental companies require drivers to be at least 21 years old, and there may be additional charges for drivers under 25.

3. Credit Card

A credit card in the primary driver's name is typically required for the rental. The card is used for the security deposit and any additional charges.

4. Insurance

Comprehensive insurance coverage is recommended. Rental companies offer various insurance options, including Collision Damage Waiver (CDW) and Theft Protection.

5. Booking in Advance
To secure the best rates and ensure vehicle availability, it's advisable to book your rental car in advance, especially during peak travel seasons.

PICKING UP YOUR RENTAL CAR
1. Airport Locations
Major international airports, including Václav Havel Airport Prague, have car rental counters conveniently located in the arrivals area.

2. City Locations
Car rental offices are also available in city centers, providing flexibility for those not arriving by air.

3. Inspection and Documentation
Before accepting the vehicle, carefully inspect it for any existing damage, and ensure that any issues are documented by the rental company.

4. GPS and Additional Equipment
Consider adding a GPS navigation system or other equipment to enhance your driving experience, especially if you plan to explore rural areas.

DRIVING IN THE CZECH REPUBLIC
1. Traffic Rules
Familiarize yourself with Czech traffic rules, which generally align with European standards. Driving is on the right side of the road.

2. Road Signs:
Pay attention to road signs, especially in rural areas where English signage may be limited.

3. Fuel Stations:

Fuel stations are widely available, and major credit cards are accepted. Unleaded petrol (Natural 95 or Natural 98) and diesel are the most common fuels.

4. Parking:

Most cities have parking zones, and it's essential to understand local parking regulations. Pay-and-display machines are common in urban areas.

EXPLORING CZECH DESTINATIONS BY CAR

1. Prague to Český Krumlov

Embark on a scenic road trip from Prague to Český Krumlov, a UNESCO-listed town known for its charming medieval architecture.

2. Bohemian Paradise (Český ráj)

Discover the stunning landscapes of Bohemian Paradise, a protected natural area featuring sandstone formations, castles, and hiking trails.

3. Moravian Wine Country
Navigate the vineyard-covered hills of South Moravia, visiting picturesque wine villages and sampling local wines.

4. Šumava National Park
Drive through Šumava National Park, a vast wilderness with dense forests, serene lakes, and diverse wildlife.

5. Karlovy Vary to Mariánské Lázně
Enjoy a scenic drive from the spa town of Karlovy Vary to Mariánské Lázně, exploring elegant architecture and relaxing spa experiences.

TIPS FOR A SMOOTH CAR RENTAL EXPERIENCE
1. Road Tolls
Be aware of road tolls on highways. The toll system is electronic, and rental cars are often equipped with an on-board unit.

2. Parking Apps
Use parking apps or maps to locate parking spaces and understand parking regulations, especially in city centers.

3. Emergency Numbers
Familiarize yourself with emergency numbers and know how to contact local authorities in case of any issues.

4. Winter Considerations
If traveling in winter, be prepared for winter driving conditions, and consider renting a car with winter tires.

5. Cultural Considerations
Respect local traffic rules and be aware of cultural nuances, such as yielding to trams and pedestrians in certain situations.

Renting a car in the Czech Republic opens up a world of possibilities, allowing you to immerse yourself in the country's diverse landscapes, historical sites, and charming towns. Whether you're cruising through the winding streets of Prague or embarking on a road trip to the scenic countryside, having your own wheels enhances the adventure and provides the flexibility to create your own unique Czech experience.

4.4 PUBLIC TRANSPORT TIPS IN THE CZECH REPUBLIC

Public transportation in the Czech Republic is a convenient and efficient way to explore cities, towns, and even neighboring regions. Whether you're taking trams, buses, or the metro, here are extensive tips to help you navigate the public transport system in the Czech Republic:

1. Integrated Ticketing System
a. City Cards:
Many cities, especially Prague, offer integrated ticketing systems that allow you to use a single ticket for trams, buses, and the metro within a specified time frame. Consider purchasing a city card for unlimited travel during your stay.

b. Ticket Validation:
Validate your ticket before boarding trams or buses. Failure to do so may result in fines. In metro stations, use your ticket to pass through the turnstile.

2. Ticket Types and Duration
a. Single Journey Tickets
Purchase single journey tickets for one-way trips. These tickets are valid for a specific duration and mode of transport.

b. Transfer Tickets

If you need to transfer between trams, buses, or metro lines, opt for transfer tickets to cover the entire journey.

c. Day and Multiple-Day Passes

For extended stays, consider day passes or multiple-day passes. These provide unlimited travel within the specified time frame.

3. Purchase Options

a. Ticket Vending Machines

Ticket vending machines are available at metro stations, tram stops, and major bus terminals. They usually accept coins and banknotes.

b. Mobile Apps

In some cities, you can purchase tickets through mobile apps, providing a convenient and contactless option.

c. Public Transport Counters

Find public transport counters at major transport hubs, where you can buy tickets and get assistance from staff.

4. Timetables and Schedules
a. Online Resources
Access online resources, including official websites and apps, to check timetables, schedules, and route maps.
b. Real-Time Information
Many cities provide real-time information at tram stops and metro stations, indicating the arrival times of the next vehicles.

5. Trams, Buses, and Metro
a. Trams
Trams are a popular mode of transport in cities like Prague and Brno. Be mindful of tram tracks when crossing streets.
b. Buses
Buses serve both urban and suburban areas. Check the bus stops for route information and schedules.
c. Metro
The metro in Prague is efficient and covers key areas. It's a quick way to travel longer distances within the city.

6. Night Transport
a. Night Trams and Buses
Some cities offer night trams and buses for late-night travel. Check the schedules, as they may run less frequently than daytime services.
b. Night Metro
Prague's metro system includes night services on certain lines. This is particularly useful for those staying out late.

7. Public Etiquette
a. Allow Exiting Passengers
When boarding trams or buses, allow exiting passengers to disembark before you board.
b. Priority Seating
Priority seating is designated for elderly passengers, pregnant women, and individuals with disabilities. Be prepared to offer these seats to those in need.

c. Quiet Zones

Some cities have designated quiet zones on trams or buses. Keep noise to a minimum in these areas.

8. Payment Methods

a. Cash and Coins

Ensure you have small change if paying with cash. Larger bills may not be accepted in ticket vending machines.

b. Contactless Payments

Where available, consider using contactless payment methods for tickets. Check if your credit card or mobile wallet is accepted.

9. Tourist Information Centers

a. Assistance for Tourists

Visit tourist information centers in major cities for guidance on public transport, maps, and any specific tourist passes available.

b. English Language Services

In tourist areas, you're likely to find English-speaking staff who can assist you with transport-related inquiries.

10. Safety and Security
a. Beware of Pickpockets
Like in any urban environment, be aware of pickpockets, especially in crowded trams and buses.

b. Emergency Contacts
Familiarize yourself with emergency contact numbers and locations of emergency exits.

11. Cultural Considerations
a. Stand on the Right
In metro stations, escalators have a convention of standing on the right side to allow those in a hurry to pass on the left.

b. Politeness and Courtesies
Embrace local customs of politeness, such as offering your seat to someone in need or saying "thank you" when exiting.

12. Accessibility
a. Wheelchair Access
Many trams and buses are equipped with ramps for wheelchair access. Check for accessible routes and vehicles.

b. Visual and Auditory Information
Efforts have been made to provide visual and auditory information at stops and stations for passengers with disabilities.

Public transport in the Czech Republic offers a cost-effective and reliable way to explore the country's urban centers and beyond. By understanding the ticketing system, embracing local etiquette, and using available resources, you'll navigate the public transport network with ease, allowing you to focus on enjoying the beauty and culture of this Central European gem.

5.0 ACCOMMODATION

5.1 HOTELS AND RESORTS IN THE CZECH REPUBLIC

Whether you seek the historic allure of Prague, the tranquility of spa towns, or the scenic retreats in the countryside, the Czech Republic offers a diverse range of hotels and resorts to suit every traveler's taste. Here's an extensive overview of accommodation options, from luxurious resorts to charming boutique hotels:

1. Prague: A Tapestry of Elegance
a. Luxury Hotels:
Iconic establishments like the Four Seasons Hotel Prague and the Augustine, a Luxury Collection Hotel, embody luxury with their

historical settings, opulent interiors, and world-class service.

b. Boutique Gems:

Embrace the charm of boutique hotels such as the Emblem Hotel or the Golden Well Hotel, nestled in the heart of Prague's Old Town. These properties offer personalized experiences in unique surroundings.

c. Modern Comfort:

For contemporary design and comfort, consider hotels like the Cosmopolitan Hotel Prague or the MOODs Boutique Hotel, providing a blend of modern amenities and architectural sophistication.

2. Spa Towns: Wellness Retreats

a. Karlovy Vary:

Experience the therapeutic ambiance of Karlovy Vary with renowned spa hotels like the Grandhotel Pupp and the Carlsbad Plaza Medical Spa & Wellness Hotel.

b. Mariánské Lázně:

Delight in the elegance of spa resorts like the Falkensteiner Hotel Grand MedSpa Marienbad or the Danubius Health Spa Resort Nové Lázně, offering relaxation in a picturesque setting.

3. Countryside Retreats: Natural Beauty Beckons
a. Český Krumlov:
Stay in charming hotels like the Hotel Ruze, housed in a former Jesuit monastery, or the Hotel Dvorak, offering views of the Vltava River and the historic town.

b. Šumava National Park:
Immerse yourself in nature with stays at eco-friendly resorts like Chata pod Lysou or charming guesthouses near Šumava National Park.

c. Moravian Wine Country:
Savor the tranquility of vineyard retreats such as the Hotel Templ in Znojmo or the Penzion U Výra in Mikulov.

4. Castles and Chateaux: Living History
a. Hluboká Castle:

Stay in the grandeur of Hluboká Castle, now a luxury hotel, and indulge in the romance of its architecture and surrounding park.
**b. Zbiroh Castle:
Experience medieval charm at Zbiroh Castle, offering unique accommodations in a historical setting.

5. Budget-Friendly Options:
a. Hostels and Guesthouses:
Explore affordable stays in hostels such as Mosaic House in Prague or opt for cozy guesthouses like Pension Alabastr in Český Krumlov.
b. Local Inns:
Discover the warmth of local inns and small hotels in towns like Telč or Kutná Hora, providing budget-friendly accommodation with a touch of authenticity.

6. Ski Resorts: Winter Wonderland Retreats

a. Špindlerův Mlýn:
Enjoy winter sports and mountain views from ski resorts like Hotel Savoy or the Hotel Horní Pramen.

b. Krkonoše Mountains:
Experience the charm of mountain retreats like Hotel Horizont in Pec pod Sněžkou, blending comfort with proximity to ski slopes.

7. Unique Stays: Memorable Experiences

a. Treehouse Stays:
Elevate your experience with treehouse accommodations, such as the Treehouse Hotel in Lipno, offering a unique blend of nature and luxury.

b. Cave Stays:
Unearth the extraordinary by staying in cave accommodations like the Caves Krasový in Moravia, providing a distinctive and immersive experience.

TRAVEL TIPS FOR ACCOMMODATIONS

1. Book in Advance:

Especially during peak seasons or festivals, secure your accommodation by booking in advance for the best availability and rates.

2. Check Reviews:

Read reviews on platforms like TripAdvisor or Booking.com to gauge the experiences of previous guests and choose accommodations that align with your preferences.

3. Cultural Sensitivity:

Embrace local customs and etiquette when staying in smaller towns or rural areas, adding a cultural touch to your experience.

4. Ask for Local Recommendations:

Consult hotel staff for local recommendations, whether it's for dining, cultural attractions, or hidden gems.

5. Explore Different Regions:
Consider diversifying your stay by exploring accommodations in various regions to capture the unique character of each destination.

The Czech Republic's hospitality landscape invites you to embark on a journey where comfort, history, and natural beauty converge. Whether you choose to indulge in the luxury of Prague's iconic hotels, rejuvenate in spa towns, or embrace the tranquility of countryside retreats, your stay in Czech hotels and resorts promises to be a memorable chapter in your travel story.

5.2 HOSTELS AND BUDGET ACCOMMODATIONS

Hostels and Budget Accommodations in the Czech Republic: Affordable Comfort for Every Explorer

For the budget-conscious traveler, the Czech Republic offers a plethora of hostels and budget accommodations that not only provide affordable stays but also contribute to a vibrant and communal travel experience. Here's an extensive guide to budget-friendly options across the country:

1. Prague: Vibrant Hostel Culture
a. Hostel One Prague:
Located in Prague's lively Žižkov district, Hostel One Prague offers a sociable atmosphere, free dinners, and daily activities to foster interaction among guests.

b. Czech Inn:
Czech Inn, situated in the Vinohrady neighborhood, combines modern design with a friendly atmosphere. It features dormitories and private rooms, catering to various traveler preferences.

c. Sophie's Hostel:
Sophie's Hostel, near Wenceslas Square, stands out with its unique design and communal spaces. The hostel organizes events, making it easy for guests to connect.

2. Český Krumlov: Quaint and Affordable Stays

a. Krumlov House:
Krumlov House, a short walk from Český Krumlov's main square, provides budget-friendly accommodation with a homely atmosphere.

b. Hostel 99:
Hostel 99 offers a central location and basic amenities, making it an ideal choice for budget travelers exploring the picturesque streets of Český Krumlov.

3. Brno: Budget Comfort in the South

a. Hostel Mitte:
Hostel Mitte, located in Brno's city center, is known for its friendly staff and proximity to attractions like Špilberk Castle.

b. Jacob Brno:
Jacob Brno, a budget-friendly hostel with a communal kitchen, is situated near the city's vibrant nightlife and cultural sites.

4. Ostrava: Affordable Urban Stays
a. Hostel u Pět'áků:
Hostel u Pět'áků in Ostrava provides economical accommodation with a cozy atmosphere, offering dormitories and private rooms.
b. Hostel Moravia Ostrava:
Hostel Moravia Ostrava is a value-for-money option, conveniently located for exploring Ostrava's industrial history and contemporary culture.

5. Plzeň: Budget Stays in the Beer Capital
a. Hostel River:
Hostel River, near the historic center of Plzeň, offers affordable dormitory-style accommodation with a focus on simplicity and comfort.
b. Hostel River View:
Hostel River View is another budget option in Plzeň, providing a convenient base for exploring the city's renowned breweries and landmarks.

6. Local Inns and Guesthouses: Authentic Charm on a Budget

a. Penzion U Zámecké Zahrady (Telč):
Enjoy the charm of Telč by staying at Penzion U Zámecké Zahrady, a local inn offering budget-friendly rooms near the town square.

b. Pension Bedrč (Kutná Hora):
Pension Bedrč in Kutná Hora provides a welcoming atmosphere and affordable accommodation, allowing guests to explore the town's historical treasures.

TRAVEL TIPS FOR BUDGET ACCOMMODATIONS:

1. Book in Advance:
Secure your budget accommodation by booking in advance, especially during peak travel seasons or events.

2. Check Amenities:
Review the amenities offered by each hostel or budget accommodation to ensure they meet your needs, whether it's Wi-Fi, communal spaces, or kitchen facilities.

3. Read Reviews:
Consult online reviews on platforms like Hostelworld or Booking.com to gauge the experiences of previous guests and select accommodations that align with your preferences.

4. Explore Shared Rooms:
Dormitory-style accommodation often comes with lower prices. Consider shared rooms to maximize savings while meeting fellow travelers.

5. Utilize Common Areas:
Take advantage of common areas in hostels for socializing and sharing travel experiences with other guests.

6. Ask Locals for Recommendations:
Seek recommendations from locals for budget-friendly accommodations that may not be listed on mainstream booking platforms.

7. Use Public Transportation:
Opt for accommodations slightly outside city centers and use public transportation to save on costs while still enjoying easy access to attractions.

Budget Exploration Awaits

From the charming streets of Prague to the historic sites of Český Krumlov and beyond, the Czech Republic's hostels and budget accommodations offer affordable comfort in the midst of cultural richness. Embrace the communal spirit of hostelling and discover the beauty of the Czech Republic without breaking the bank.

5.3 UNIQUE STAYS AND BOUTIQUE HOTELS IN CZECH REPUBLIC

For travelers seeking an extraordinary and personalized experience, the Czech Republic offers a collection of unique stays and boutique hotels. From historic palaces to whimsical treehouses, these accommodations combine distinctive design with attentive service to create memorable stays. Here's an extensive guide to discovering the charm of boutique stays across the country:

1. Prague: A Tapestry of Boutique Elegance

a. Ventana Hotel Prague:

Nestled in the heart of Prague's Old Town, Ventana Hotel Prague exudes sophistication with its blend of classic and contemporary design. Enjoy views of the historic surroundings and personalized service.

b. Golden Well Hotel:

Overlooking Prague Castle, Golden Well Hotel offers a luxurious retreat in a beautifully restored Renaissance building. Indulge in elegant rooms and a peaceful terrace with panoramic views.

c. Aria Hotel Prague:
Aria Hotel Prague, adjacent to the iconic Prague Castle, is a music-themed boutique hotel. Each room represents a different music genre, providing a unique and artistic ambiance.

2. Český Krumlov: Charming Boutique Retreats
a. Hotel Ruze:
Housed in a former Jesuit monastery, Hotel Ruze in Český Krumlov combines historic charm with modern amenities. Its unique architecture and riverside location make for an enchanting stay.

b. Hotel Dvorak:
Situated on the banks of the Vltava River, Hotel Dvorak offers panoramic views of Český Krumlov. The hotel's historic atmosphere and stylish interiors create a captivating environment.

3. Brno: Boutique Elegance in the South
a. Barceló Brno Palace:
Barceló Brno Palace, located in Brno's city center, boasts a neo-Renaissance façade and

contemporary interiors. Its luxurious rooms and fine dining restaurant contribute to a refined stay.

b. Kings Court Boutique Hotel:
Kings Court Boutique Hotel, a short walk from Brno's main square, combines modern design with Art Deco elements. Experience personalized service and sophisticated accommodations.

4. Karlovy Vary: Spa Luxury in Boutique Form
a. Quisisana Palace:
Quisisana Palace in Karlovy Vary exudes elegance with its Belle Époque architecture and luxurious interiors. The boutique hotel offers a tranquil retreat in the heart of the spa town.

b. Grandhotel Pupp:
Grandhotel Pupp, an iconic hotel in Karlovy Vary, blends historic grandeur with modern comfort. The hotel's spa facilities and grand dining venues add to its timeless appeal.

5. Treehouse Stays: Elevated Comfort in Nature
a. Treehouse Hotel Lipno:
Experience a unique stay at Treehouse Hotel Lipno, situated near Lake Lipno. These elevated accommodations provide a perfect blend of comfort and immersion in nature.

6. Castle Stays: Living History
a. Hluboká Castle:
Hluboká Castle, transformed into a luxury hotel, offers a regal experience. Stay in beautifully appointed rooms surrounded by the enchanting atmosphere of the castle.

b. Zbiroh Castle:
Zbiroh Castle provides a medieval-inspired stay with elegant rooms and period furnishings. This unique setting allows guests to step back in time while enjoying modern comforts.

7. Cave Stays: Subterranean Serenity
a. Caves Krasový (Moravia):
Discover the extraordinary by staying in underground caves at Caves Krasový in Moravia. These unique accommodations offer a

one-of-a-kind experience surrounded by natural beauty.

TRAVEL TIPS FOR BOUTIQUE STAYS:

1. Book in Advance:
As boutique hotels often have limited rooms, it's advisable to book in advance, especially during peak travel seasons or events.

2. Explore Unique Features:
Choose boutique stays that align with your interests. Whether it's themed rooms, historic

charm, or natural surroundings, boutique hotels often offer distinctive features.

3. Contact the Hotel Directly:
Reach out to the hotel directly to inquire about special packages, personalized experiences, or any unique offerings that may enhance your stay.

4. Take Advantage of Local Recommendations:
Boutique hotel staff are often well-connected to local attractions and hidden gems. Seek their recommendations for authentic experiences.

5. Read Guest Reviews:
Before booking, read guest reviews to gain insights into the personalized service, design elements, and overall experience provided by the boutique hotel.

Boutique Splendor Beckons
Indulge in the charm and elegance of boutique stays across the Czech Republic, where each

property is a testament to personalized service and distinctive design. Whether you're drawn to the historic allure of Prague or the tranquil landscapes of Český Krumlov, these boutique accommodations promise a unique and enchanting experience, making your journey through the Czech Republic truly memorable.

6.0 CUISINE

6.1 TRADITIONAL CZECH DISHES: CULINARY DELIGHTS FROM THE HEART OF EUROPE

The Czech Republic boasts a rich culinary heritage, with traditional dishes that reflect the country's history, culture, and agricultural abundance. From hearty meats to savory dumplings and sweet delights, Czech cuisine invites you to savor the flavors of Central Europe. Here's an extensive exploration of some iconic traditional Czech dishes:

1. Svíčková na Smetaně (Marinated Beef Sirloin):

Description: A classic Czech dish, Svíčková na Smetaně features marinated beef sirloin served with a creamy sauce. The meat is marinated in a mixture of vegetables, spices, and a hint of vinegar, then slow-cooked to perfection.

Accompaniments:
Creamy Sauce: Made with sour cream, root vegetables, and a touch of mustard, the sauce is integral to the dish's rich flavor.
Bread Dumplings (Knedlíky): Sliced and served alongside the meat, these dumplings absorb the delicious sauce.

2. Guláš (Goulash):
Description: Guláš, a beloved dish across Central Europe, is a hearty stew made with tender beef or pork, onions, and paprika. It's slow-cooked to achieve a robust flavor, and variations may include potatoes or other vegetables.

Accompaniments:
Bread or Dumplings: Guláš is often served with slices of fresh bread or dumplings to soak up the flavorful sauce.

3. Trdelník (Chimney Cake):

Description: While not exclusive to the Czech Republic, Trdelník is a popular street food and dessert. This cylindrical pastry is made by wrapping dough around a spindle, grilling it until golden, and coating it in a mixture of sugar and cinnamon.

Variations:

Filled Trdelník: Some vendors offer filled variations with ice cream, whipped cream, or Nutella for added indulgence.

4. Koleno (Pork Knee):

Description: Koleno is a pork knee roast, slow-cooked until the skin is crispy, and the meat is tender. This dish is a staple in Czech beer gardens and pubs, often accompanied by mustard and horseradish.

Accompaniments:

Pickled Vegetables: Served as a refreshing contrast to the rich, savory pork.

5. Vepřo-knedlo-zelo (Roast Pork with Dumplings and Sauerkraut):

Description: Vepřo-knedlo-zelo is a quintessential Czech dish, featuring roast pork accompanied by bread dumplings and sauerkraut. The combination of savory pork, fluffy dumplings, and tangy sauerkraut creates a harmonious culinary experience.

Accompaniments:
Gravy: A flavorful gravy often drizzled over the roast pork and dumplings.

6. Smažený Sýr (Fried Cheese):

Description: Smažený Sýr is a popular snack or light meal, consisting of deep-fried cheese, typically Edam or Emmental. The cheese is coated in breadcrumbs, fried until golden brown, and served with a side of tartar sauce.

Serving Style:
Sandwich Form: Smažený Sýr is sometimes served in a bun with condiments like mayonnaise and ketchup.

7. Cibulák (Onion Soup):

Description: Cibulák is a comforting onion soup made with caramelized onions, broth, and sometimes beer. It is topped with toasted bread and melted cheese, creating a warm and savory dish.

Flavor Enhancers:
Garlic: Some recipes include garlic for an extra layer of flavor in the broth.

8. Palačinky (Czech Pancakes):

Description: Palačinky are thin Czech pancakes similar to crêpes. They can be enjoyed in various ways, whether filled with jam, Nutella, or a mixture of fruits, and are often dusted with powdered sugar.

Popular Fillings:
Fruit Compote: Palačinky are sometimes served with a warm fruit compote for added sweetness

9. Kulajda (Creamy Dill Soup):

Description: Kulajda is a traditional Czech soup featuring a creamy base, potatoes, mushrooms, dill, and a poached egg. The combination of flavors creates a unique and satisfying soup.

Ingredients:

Sour Cream: Sour cream is a key component, giving the soup its creamy texture and a slightly tangy flavor.

10. Medovník (Honey Cake):

Description: Medovník is a layered honey cake with sweet and spiced layers of sponge cake, often filled with a rich cream or frosting. It's a delightful dessert enjoyed during celebrations and special occasions.

Decorations:

Walnuts or Almonds: Some variations of Medovník are adorned with crushed walnuts or almonds for added texture.

A Feast for the Senses

Czech cuisine offers a diverse array of dishes that reflect the country's agricultural traditions and culinary creativity. Whether you're savoring the tender beef of Svíčková, indulging in the comforting warmth of Guláš, or treating yourself to the sweet layers of Medovník, the traditional dishes of the Czech Republic promise a feast for the senses, inviting you to explore the rich tapestry of flavors from the heart of Europe.

6.2 POPULAR RESTAURANTS AND CAFÉS IN THE CZECH REPUBLIC

The Czech Republic, with its rich culinary traditions, boasts a vibrant food scene that caters to diverse tastes. From historic restaurants serving traditional Czech dishes to modern cafés with international influences, here's an extensive exploration of some popular establishments that define the gastronomic landscape of the Czech Republic:

1. Lokál: A Taste of Authentic Pilsner Culture
Location: Various locations, including Prague and Pilsen.

Description: Lokál, with its warm and convivial atmosphere, offers a genuine Czech pub experience. Known for serving Pilsner Urquell beer straight from the tank, Lokál complements its beer selection with classic Czech dishes like svíčková and hearty goulash.

Signature Dish:
Beef Tartare: Lokál is renowned for its deliciously seasoned beef tartare, a favorite among locals and visitors alike.

2. La Degustation Bohême Bourgeoise:
Michelin-Starred Czech Cuisine
Location: Prague

Description: La Degustation Bohême Bourgeoise is a Michelin-starred restaurant that takes guests on a journey through Czech gastronomy. With an emphasis on traditional recipes and high-quality ingredients, the tasting menu offers an exquisite experience showcasing the depth of Czech flavors.

Signature Dish:

Beef in Cream Sauce (Svíčková): La Degustation's interpretation of this classic Czech dish is a refined and elegant rendition.

3. Kavárna Slavia: A Historic Café with a View

Location: Prague

Description: Situated near the National Theatre, Kavárna Slavia is a historic café that has been a hub for artists and intellectuals for over a century. With its grand interiors and views of the Vltava River, it's an ideal spot for coffee, desserts, or a leisurely meal.

Must-Try:

Apple Strudel (Jablečný Závin): Pair your coffee with a slice of Kavárna Slavia's delicious apple strudel.

4. Mincovna: Fusion of Czech and International Flavors

Location: Prague

Description: Mincovna, located in the heart of Prague, offers a fusion of Czech and international cuisines. The restaurant's contemporary design and diverse menu attract both locals and tourists looking for a modern twist on traditional flavors.

Recommended Dish:
Duck Confit Burger: Experience a delightful blend of Czech and international flavors with Mincovna's inventive duck confit burger.

5. Café Louvre: A Bohemian Gem with Literary History

Location: Prague

Description: Café Louvre, a historic café with roots dating back to 1902, has hosted literary figures like Franz Kafka. Renovated to its former glory, it combines a nostalgic atmosphere with a diverse menu, offering breakfast, lunch, and dinner options.

Specialty Treat:

Traditional Czech Pancakes: Indulge in Café Louvre's delightful Czech pancakes, either sweet or savory, for a satisfying culinary experience.

6. Vinohradský Pivovar: Craft Beer and Culinary Excellence

Location: Prague

Description: Vinohradský Pivovar is not just a craft brewery; it's also a destination for excellent Czech cuisine. With a selection of craft beers brewed on-site and a menu featuring both traditional and modern dishes, it provides a dynamic culinary experience.

Highlight:

Beer Tasting Flight: Explore the brewery's diverse beer offerings with a tasting flight, perfectly paired with hearty Czech dishes.

7. Café Savoy: A Blend of Elegance and Gastronomy

Location: Prague

Description: Café Savoy, located in a stunning Art Nouveau building, combines elegance with a menu that celebrates both Czech and French culinary traditions. Its historic charm, attentive

service, and delectable pastries make it a must-visit.
Exquisite Dessert:
Savoy Cake: Treat yourself to the signature Savoy Cake, a layered delight that reflects the café's commitment to craftsmanship.

8. Ambiente Pizza Nuova: Authentic Italian Flavors in Prague
Location: Prague

Description: Ambiente Pizza Nuova brings authentic Italian flavors to Prague. With a focus on quality ingredients and traditional pizza-making techniques, this pizzeria has earned a reputation for serving some of the best pizza in the city.
Highly Recommended:
Margherita Pizza: Experience the simplicity and perfection of a classic Margherita pizza prepared with top-notch ingredients.

9. Kolkovna Olympia: A Czech Beer Hall Experience

Location: Prague

Description: Kolkovna Olympia captures the essence of a traditional Czech beer hall. With a wide selection of beers, hearty dishes, and a lively atmosphere, it's a favorite among locals and visitors seeking an authentic pub experience.

Beer Connoisseur's Choice:

Pilsner Urquell on Tap: Enjoy the crisp and refreshing taste of Pilsner Urquell straight from the tap, a quintessential Czech beer experience.

10. Mlejnice: Bohemian Charm and Hearty Fare

Location: Prague

Description: Mlejnice, nestled in the historic Old Town, offers Bohemian charm and a menu filled with hearty Czech dishes. The rustic setting and generous portions make it a favorite for those seeking a traditional Czech dining experience.

Generous Portion to Share:

Roasted Pork Knuckle (Vepřové Koleno): Gather friends and indulge in a shared feast with Mlejnice's succulent roasted pork knuckle.

A Feast for Every Palate

From historic cafés with literary legacies to Michelin-starred establishments, the Czech Republic's culinary landscape invites you to embark on a gastronomic journey. Whether you're savoring the refined creations at La Degustation Bohême Bourgeoise or relishing the comforting atmosphere of Lokál, each restaurant and café contributes to the diverse tapestry of flavors that define the heart of Europe. Whether you're a connoisseur of traditional Czech dishes or seeking innovative culinary experiences, the Czech Republic offers a feast for every palate.

6.3 FOOD FESTIVALS AND EVENTS IN THE CZECH REPUBLIC

The Czech Republic, with its rich culinary traditions, hosts a variety of food festivals and events throughout the year. These gatherings celebrate the diversity of Czech cuisine, showcase local and international flavors, and provide a platform for food enthusiasts to come together. Here's an extensive exploration of some notable food festivals and events in the Czech Republic

1. Prague Food Festival: A Culinary Extravaganza in the Capital
Location: Prague

Description: The Prague Food Festival is a highlight on the city's culinary calendar, attracting foodies and chefs alike. Held in picturesque venues, this gastronomic event features renowned chefs presenting their signature dishes, cooking demonstrations, and a vibrant atmosphere celebrating the best of Czech and international cuisine.

Highlights:

Tasting Menus: Visitors can indulge in tasting menus from top restaurants, showcasing a diverse array of flavors and culinary techniques.

Wine Tasting: The festival often includes wine tastings, allowing attendees to pair exquisite dishes with fine wines.

2. Beer Festivals: A Toast to Czech Brewing Heritage

Locations: Various cities, including Prague, Pilsen, and České Budějovice.

Description: The Czech Republic, known as the birthplace of Pilsner lager, celebrates its brewing heritage with numerous beer festivals. Events like the Pilsner Fest in Pilsen and the Czech Beer Festival in Prague offer a chance to savor a wide range of Czech beers, from traditional lagers to innovative craft brews.

Key Features:

Beer Tastings: Visitors can explore a vast selection of Czech beers, including those from local microbreweries.

Beer Competitions: Some festivals host beer competitions, where breweries showcase their best brews for judging.

3. Znojmo Historical Vintage: Wine and Gastronomy in South Moravia

Location: Znojmo

Description: Znojmo Historical Vintage is a celebration of South Moravia's wine culture, featuring a blend of wine, history, and gastronomy. Held in the historic town of

Znojmo, the event includes wine tastings, culinary demonstrations, and a medieval fair, transporting attendees to a bygone era.

Key Elements:
Wine Tastings: Visitors can sample a wide range of Moravian wines, known for their distinct flavors and high quality.
Culinary Offerings: Local restaurants and vendors showcase regional specialties to complement the wine experience.

4. Kutná Hora Feast: A Medieval Culinary Journey
Location: Kutná Hora

Description: The Kutná Hora Feast takes participants on a journey back in time to the medieval era. Held in the historic setting of Kutná Hora, this event features period costumes, live music, and a feast inspired by medieval recipes, providing a unique culinary and cultural experience.

Notable Elements:

Medieval Banquet: Attendees can partake in a banquet inspired by historical recipes, complete with traditional dishes and entertainment.

Craftsmanship Demonstrations: The festival often includes demonstrations of medieval crafts, enhancing the immersive experience.

5. Cheese Markets: Celebrating Czech Dairy Delights

Locations: Various cities and towns

Description: Cheese markets are a popular feature in many Czech cities and towns, celebrating the country's dairy traditions. These events showcase a variety of local cheeses, artisanal products, and culinary creations centered around this beloved ingredient.

Highlights:

Cheese Tastings: Attendees can sample and purchase a diverse range of Czech cheeses, including regional specialties.

Cooking Demonstrations: Chefs often demonstrate creative ways to incorporate cheese into both savory and sweet dishes.

6. Street Food Festivals: Global Flavors in a Local Setting

Locations: Various cities, including Prague, Brno, and Ostrava

Description: Street food festivals have gained popularity in Czech cities, bringing together food trucks, vendors, and culinary enthusiasts. These festivals celebrate international street food flavors while providing a platform for local chefs and food entrepreneurs.

Features:

Diverse Cuisine: Street food festivals offer a smorgasbord of global cuisines, allowing visitors to explore flavors from different corners of the world.

Live Music and Entertainment: Many festivals include live music performances and entertainment to enhance the lively atmosphere.

7. Chocofest: A Sweet Celebration of Chocolate
Location: Prague
Description: Chocofest is a paradise for chocolate lovers, showcasing the finest chocolates from Czech and international chocolatiers. The event features chocolate tastings, workshops, and a chance to indulge in an array of chocolate creations.
Sweet Highlights:
Chocolate Tastings: Attendees can explore a wide range of chocolates, from traditional pralines to innovative chocolate-infused desserts.
Masterclasses: Chocofest often includes masterclasses where participants can learn about the art of chocolate making.

8. Moravian Autumn: Harvest Celebrations in South Moravia
Location: Various towns in South Moravia
Description: Moravian Autumn, or Moravský Podzim, is a series of events celebrating the autumn harvest in South Moravia. Alongside traditional folklore and cultural activities, the

festival features food markets, wine tastings, and culinary events highlighting the region's seasonal produce.

Harvest Delights:

Wine Trails: Explore wine trails featuring tastings of the new wine harvest, a significant tradition in the Moravian wine region.

Local Produce Markets: Attendees can purchase fresh produce, regional specialties, and artisanal products from local vendors.

9. Brno Food Festival: Showcasing Culinary Diversity

Location: Brno

Description: The Brno Food Festival is an annual event that celebrates the diverse culinary scene in and around Brno. It brings together local restaurants, chefs, and food enthusiasts for a weekend of tastings, cooking demonstrations, and gastronomic experiences.

Event Highlights:

Gourmet Tastings: Visitors can sample dishes from a variety of local restaurants, showcasing the culinary talent in the region.

Chef Competitions: The festival often includes competitions where chefs demonstrate their skills and creativity.

10. Pardubice Gingerbread Festival: Sweet Creations in Eastern Bohemia
Location: pardubice
Description: The Pardubice Gingerbread Festival celebrates the art of gingerbread making, a tradition deeply rooted in the region's history. Visitors can enjoy gingerbread tastings, witness gingerbread competitions, and explore the creativity of local bakers.

Gingerbread Artistry:
Gingerbread Workshops: Attendees can participate in gingerbread decorating workshops and create their sweet masterpieces.
Gingerbread Sculptures: The festival often features impressive gingerbread sculptures and artistic displays.

Conclusion: A Culinary Journey Across Regions

From the beer-centric celebrations of Pilsner Fest to the medieval feasts in Kutná Hora, the Czech Republic's food festivals and events offer a diverse and delightful culinary journey. Whether you're sipping wine in Znoj

7.0 CULTURAL EXPERIENCES

7.1 FESTIVALS AND CELEBRATIONS IN THE CZECH REPUBLIC: A TAPESTRY OF CULTURE AND TRADITION

The Czech Republic, nestled in the heart of Europe, is a land of vibrant festivals and celebrations that reflect its rich history, cultural diversity, and the spirit of its people. From traditional folk festivals to modern music extravaganzas, each event contributes to the colorful tapestry of Czech life. Here's an extensive exploration of some of the most significant festivals and celebrations in the Czech Republic:

1. Prague Spring International Music Festival: A Symphony of Classical Excellence
Location: Prague

Description: The Prague Spring International Music Festival is a renowned classical music event held annually in the Czech capital. Established in 1946, it attracts top orchestras, conductors, and soloists from around the world. The festival's venues, including the iconic Rudolfinum and Municipal House, provide a majestic backdrop for performances.

Highlights:
Orchestral Concerts: Internationally acclaimed orchestras showcase masterpieces from classical repertoire, captivating audiences with their virtuosity.
Chamber Music Performances: The festival includes intimate chamber music concerts, allowing attendees to experience the nuanced artistry of smaller ensembles.

2. Karlovy Vary International Film
Festival: A Cinematic Extravaganza
Location: Karlovy Vary

Description: The Karlovy Vary International Film Festival, one of the oldest film festivals in the world, celebrates cinema in the picturesque spa town of Karlovy Vary. Established in 1946, it has become a prominent platform for showcasing international and Czech films, attracting filmmakers, actors, and cinephiles from across the globe.

Event Highlights:

Film Screenings: The festival features a diverse selection of films, including premieres, documentaries, and works by emerging filmmakers.

Red Carpet Events: Glamorous red carpet events and award ceremonies add a touch of Hollywood-style excitement to the festival.

3. Czech Beer Festival: Cheers to Beer Culture

Location: Prague

Description: The Czech Beer Festival, held in Prague, is a celebration of the country's brewing heritage. With an extensive selection of Czech beers, traditional cuisine, and lively entertainment, it provides a festive atmosphere for locals and visitors alike.

Festival Features:
Beer Tents: Numerous beer tents showcase a variety of Czech beers, including well-known lagers and craft brews.
Culinary Delights: Festival-goers can savor traditional Czech dishes, such as grilled sausages, roasted pork, and dumplings.

4. Masopust (Carnival): A Colorful Folk Tradition
Location: Various towns and villages
Description: Masopust, the Czech Carnival, is a lively pre-Lenten celebration with roots in pagan and Christian traditions. Participants don elaborate masks and costumes, take part in processions, and indulge in merrymaking before the Lenten season begins.
Carnival Elements:

Masked Parades: Towns and villages come alive with vibrant parades featuring participants in colorful masks and costumes.

Traditional Music and Dance: Masopust celebrations often include folk music, dancing, and festivities in the streets.

5. Easter Markets: Welcoming Spring with Tradition

Locations: Various cities, including Prague and Brno

Description: Easter markets in the Czech Republic are a charming way to welcome the arrival of spring. These markets showcase traditional Easter decorations, handcrafted goods, and local delicacies, creating a festive atmosphere in city squares.

Market Highlights:

Easter Decorations: Artisans offer intricately decorated eggs, traditional handcrafted items, and festive decorations.

Easter Treats: Market-goers can sample Easter sweets, pastries, and other seasonal delights.

6. St. Nicholas Day: A Magical Evening for Families
Location: Nationwide
Description: St. Nicholas Day, celebrated on December 6th, is a beloved tradition in the Czech Republic. Families come together for a magical evening when St. Nicholas, accompanied by an angel and a devil, visits homes to reward well-behaved children with sweets and small gifts.
Festive Elements:
St. Nicholas Processions: In many towns and cities, processions featuring St. Nicholas, angels, and devils entertain families with festive performances.
Gift-Giving: St. Nicholas presents small gifts and sweets to children who have been good throughout the year.

7. Czech Independence Day: Honoring National Identity
Location: Nationwide

Description: Czech Independence Day, celebrated on October 28th, commemorates the founding of Czechoslovakia in 1918. The day is marked by various events, including patriotic ceremonies, cultural activities, and exhibitions highlighting the nation's history.

National Pride:

Flag Ceremonies: Events often include flag-raising ceremonies, where the national flag is proudly displayed.

Cultural Exhibitions: Museums and cultural institutions may organize exhibitions showcasing key moments in Czech history.

8. Mikuláš (St. Nicholas) Celebrations: A Winter Tradition

Location: Nationwide

Description: Mikuláš, or St. Nicholas, celebrations take place on the evening of December 5th. Accompanied by an angel and a devil, St. Nicholas visits homes, schools, and public spaces to reward children for their behavior during the year.

Mikuláš Processions:

Community Events: Towns and villages organize processions featuring Mikuláš, the angel, and the devil, providing festive entertainment for residents.

Gift-Giving: St. Nicholas gives small gifts and treats to children, while the devil may playfully tease them for any mischievous behavior.

9. Becherovka Folklore Festival: A Celebration of Bohemian Culture

Location: Karlovy Vary

Description: The Becherovka Folklore Festival, named after the famous Czech herbal liqueur, celebrates Bohemian folklore and traditions. Held

7.2 MUSEUM AND GALLERIES

The Czech Republic, with its rich history and artistic heritage, hosts a diverse array of museums and galleries that showcase the country's cultural wealth. From world-class art collections to immersive museums and galleries historical exhibits, these institutions provide visitors with a captivating journey through the centuries. Here's an extensive exploration of some of the notable museums and galleries in the Czech Republic:

1. National Museum (Národní Muzeum): A Cultural Chronicle in Prague
Location: Prague
Description: The National Museum in Prague stands as a cultural beacon, encompassing a wide range of disciplines, including history, natural sciences, arts, and music. The museum's imposing building on Wenceslas Square is an architectural landmark, and its collections offer a comprehensive exploration of Czech heritage.
Highlighted Collections:

Historical Exhibits: The museum's historical exhibits delve into the evolution of Czech lands, from prehistory to the present day.

Natural History Hall: Discover the wonders of the natural world, including fossils, minerals, and taxidermy specimens.

2. Prague Castle Galleries: Artistic Majesty in the Heart of the City

Location: Prague Castle

Description: The Prague Castle complex not only boasts historical significance but also houses galleries that showcase art spanning various periods. From Gothic and Renaissance masterpieces to contemporary works, the galleries within Prague Castle offer a visual feast against the backdrop of stunning architecture.

Galleries Within the Castle:

Old Royal Palace Gallery: Featuring Gothic and Renaissance art, including the impressive Vladislav Hall.

Convent of St. George Gallery: Showcasing Romanesque and Gothic art, including the St. George Basilica.

3. National Gallery In Prague: Artistic Panorama Across Centuries

Location: Various locations, including Prague and Šternberk

Description: The National Gallery in Prague is a treasure trove of art, spread across multiple locations. From medieval icons to contemporary installations, the gallery's diverse collections provide insight into the evolution of Czech and European art.

Prominent Locations:

Veletržní Palace: Home to modern and contemporary art, including works by Czech and international artists.

Convent of St. Agnes of Bohemia: A medieval setting featuring Gothic art and a tranquil garden.

4. DOX Centre for Contemporary Art: A Hub of Innovation

Location: Prague

Description: The DOX Centre for Contemporary Art is a dynamic space that fosters creativity and showcases cutting-edge contemporary art. With a focus on interdisciplinary projects, the center invites visitors to engage with thought-provoking exhibitions and participate in discussions about the intersection of art and society.

Notable Features:
Rotating Exhibitions: DOX hosts a diverse range of exhibitions, spanning visual arts, design, architecture, and multimedia installations.
Educational Programs: The center offers educational initiatives, workshops, and events that promote artistic dialogue and exploration.

5. Moravská Galerie (Moravian Gallery) in Brno: Art Oasis in Moravia
Location: Brno
Description: The Moravian Gallery in Brno is a cultural hub in Moravia, featuring an extensive collection of fine arts, applied arts, and design. The gallery's venues, including the Governor's

Palace and the Pražák Palace, provide an elegant setting for artistic exploration.
Showcased Artistic Movements:

Czech Modernism: Explore the works of Czech modernist artists, including paintings, sculptures, and decorative arts.
Contemporary Art: The gallery actively engages with contemporary art, supporting emerging artists and showcasing innovative projects.

6. The Alfons Mucha Museum: A Tribute to Art Nouveau
Location: Prague
Description: Dedicated to the iconic Art Nouveau artist Alfons Mucha, this museum in Prague celebrates the life and work of the renowned Czech painter and decorative artist. The museum displays a comprehensive collection of Mucha's paintings, posters, and decorative arts.

Key Features:

Mucha's Masterpieces: View iconic works such as "The Slav Epic" and "The Mucha Window," as well as posters and decorative items.

Interactive Exhibits: Engage with interactive displays that offer insights into Mucha's artistic process and the Art Nouveau movement.

7. Lobkowicz Palace: Private Collections Unveiled

Location: Prague Castle

Description: The Lobkowicz Palace, located within Prague Castle, houses one of the most significant private art collections in Central Europe. As the only privately owned building in Prague Castle, it offers visitors a glimpse into the history and cultural legacy of the Lobkowicz family.

Showcased Collections:

Fine Arts: Explore a vast array of European paintings,

7.3 HARMONY AND EXPRESSION: PERFORMING ARTS AND MUSIC IN THE CZECH REPUBLIC

The Czech Republic, a cultural crossroads in the heart of Europe, has fostered a rich legacy in the performing arts and music. From classical compositions that echo through historic concert halls to contemporary expressions of creativity in theaters and festivals, the Czech cultural landscape is a vibrant tapestry of artistic endeavors. Here's an extensive exploration of the performing arts and music in the Czech Republic:

1. Classical Music and the Czech Philharmonic: A Symphony of Excellence

Ensemble: Czech Philharmonic Orchestra

Description: The Czech Philharmonic Orchestra, founded in 1896, stands as a pillar of Czech classical music. Renowned for its exceptional musicianship, the orchestra has contributed significantly to the global classical music scene. Prague's Rudolfinum serves as its principal concert venue, hosting captivating performances of works by Czech and international composers.

Notable Composers:

Antonín Dvořák: A celebrated Czech composer whose symphonies, chamber music, and operas are cornerstones of the classical repertoire.

Bedřich Smetana: Known for his symphonic poem "Ma Vlast" and the opera "The Bartered Bride," Smetana is a key figure in Czech music.

2. National Theatre (Národní Divadlo): A Theatrical Jewel in Prague

Location: Prague

Description: The National Theatre in Prague, a symbol of Czech national identity, encompasses multiple artistic disciplines, including opera, drama, and ballet. Its historical stages, such as the Czech, New, and State Opera, provide a platform for both classic and contemporary performances.

Highlights: Opera Performances: The National Theatre stages a repertoire of operas, featuring both Czech and international productions.

Dramatic Arts: The Drama and Ballet ensembles contribute to a diverse program that spans from classical plays to avant-garde productions.

3. Janáček Opera in Brno: Celebrating Czech Opera

Location: Brno

Description: The Janáček Opera, part of the National Theatre Brno, specializes in the works of Czech composer Leoš Janáček. The opera company contributes to the preservation and promotion of Czech operatic heritage, staging productions that showcase Janáček's distinctive style and thematic exploration.

Key Productions:

"Jenůfa": This opera, exploring themes of love, betrayal, and redemption, is one of Janáček's most renowned works.

"The Cunning Little Vixen": A whimsical opera that weaves together human and animal characters in a narrative inspired by a comic strip.

4. Festivals: Melodic Celebrations Across the Country
Notable Festivals:

Prague Spring International Music Festival: An annual celebration of classical music, featuring international orchestras, conductors, and soloists.

Colours of Ostrava: A multi-genre music festival set in an industrial landscape, showcasing diverse artists from the realms of rock, indie, electronic, and world music.

5. Czech Jazz Scene: Syncopated Rhythms and Improvisations

Description: The Czech jazz scene, deeply rooted in the country's musical tradition, has flourished with a blend of innovation and appreciation for diverse styles. Jazz clubs in cities like Prague and Brno provide platforms for both local and international jazz musicians to showcase their talents.

Prominent Jazz Figures:

Emil Viklický: A highly regarded Czech jazz pianist and composer, known for his contributions to the international jazz scene.

Jiří Stivín: A versatile musician proficient in multiple instruments, Stivín has left an indelible mark on the Czech jazz landscape.

6. Kutná Hora Music Festival: A Cultural Resonance in a Historic Setting
Location: Kutná Hora

Description: The Kutná Hora Music Festival offers a unique blend of classical, jazz, and contemporary music within the captivating historical setting of Kutná Hora. This annual festival attracts both local and international performers, creating a cultural convergence that resonates through the medieval town.

Musical Diversity:

Classical Concerts: The festival presents classical concerts in churches and historic venues, enhancing the musical experience with architectural beauty.

Contemporary Performances: Jazz, world music, and contemporary compositions contribute to the festival's eclectic program.

7. Rock for People: A Rock and Indie Extravaganza
Location: Hradec Králové

Description: Rock for People is one of the largest music festivals in the Czech Republic, drawing music enthusiasts from various genres. With a focus on rock, indie, and electronic music, the festival features international headliners and emerging artists, creating a dynamic atmosphere of musical exploration.

Festival Elements:

Diverse Stages: Multiple stages host performances ranging from rock and indie to electronic and alternative music.

Camping Community: The festival's camping area fosters a sense of community, allowing attendees to immer

7.4 LOCAL TRADITIONS AND CUSTOMS IN THE REPUBLIC

The Czech Republic, nestled in the heart of Europe, boasts a rich tapestry of traditions and customs that reflect its historical and cultural heritage. From festive celebrations to time-honored rituals, these customs provide insight into the unique identity of the Czech people. Here's an exploration of some notable local traditions and customs:

1. Easter Monday: Whipping and Watering Tradition

Description: Easter Monday, known as "Pomlázka" in Czech, is marked by a unique tradition where boys and men playfully whip girls and women with handmade whips called "pomlázka." This custom is believed to bring health, vitality, and fertility to the women. In return, women give men colored eggs and sometimes reward them with sweets or shots of plum brandy.

Symbolic Elements:

Whipping Ritual: The gentle whipping is more symbolic than forceful, emphasizing the renewal of life and the arrival of spring.

Watering Tradition: In some regions, it is also customary to splash or pour water on women, signifying purification and rejuvenation.

2. St. Nicholas Day (Mikuláš): A Winter Tradition

Description: St. Nicholas Day, celebrated on December 5th, involves a procession featuring St. Nicholas, an angel, and a devil. St. Nicholas visits homes, schools, and public spaces to reward well-behaved children with sweets and small gifts. The devil may playfully tease children, creating a festive and theatrical atmosphere.

Festive Elements:

Costumed Processions: St. Nicholas is often accompanied by individuals dressed as an angel and a devil, adding a whimsical touch to the festivities.

Gift-Giving: St. Nicholas distributes sweets, chocolates, and small presents to children who have behaved well during the year.

3. Maypole (Májový Stromeček): Welcoming Spring

Description: The Maypole tradition, known as "májový stromeček," is a springtime custom celebrated on May 1st. In villages and towns, a tall pole adorned with ribbons, flowers, and greenery is erected. The Maypole symbolizes the arrival of spring, and communities often gather for festivities, dances, and the raising of the Maypole.

Community Celebrations:
Maypole Decorating: Local communities come together to decorate the Maypole with colorful ribbons, flowers, and sometimes painted symbols.
Dancing and Festivities: Maypole celebrations include traditional dances, music, and communal activities that foster a sense of togetherness.

4. Christmas Traditions: Carp and Midnight Mass
Description: Christmas in the Czech Republic is marked by unique customs, including the preparation of a festive meal centered around carp and the attendance of Midnight Mass. Carp

is a traditional Christmas dish, often purchased alive and kept in the bathtub before being prepared for the holiday feast.

Christmas Rituals:

Carp Preparation: Families often purchase live carp, which is kept in the bathtub until Christmas Eve when it is cooked and served as a main dish.

Midnight Mass: Many Czechs attend Midnight Mass (Půlnoční Mše) on Christmas Eve, marking the beginning of the Christmas celebrations.

5. Czech Folk Music and Dance: A Living Tradition

Description: Folk music and dance play a significant role in Czech cultural heritage. Traditional folk ensembles, often featuring colorful costumes and lively choreography, showcase regional variations of Czech folk traditions. Festivals and events celebrate this living tradition, providing a platform for folk artists to share their heritage.

Distinctive Features:

Costumes: Folk dancers wear region-specific costumes adorned with intricate embroidery, reflecting the diversity of Czech folk traditions.

Musical Instruments: Traditional Czech folk music often incorporates instruments like the accordion, violin, and clarinet, creating a lively and rhythmic sound.

6. Czech Beer Culture: Toasts and Socializing

Description: The Czech Republic has a strong beer culture, and toasting with beer is a common social custom. Beer is an integral part of Czech social life, and gatherings often revolve around sharing stories, laughter, and toasts.

Beer Etiquette:

Toasting Phrases: When toasting, it's common to say "Na zdraví!" meaning "To your health!" as a gesture of goodwill.

Socializing in Pubs: Pubs and beer gardens serve as social hubs, where friends and colleagues gather for relaxed conversations over a pint of beer.

7. Czech Cuisine and Culinary Traditions

Description: Czech cuisine is deeply rooted in tradition, featuring hearty and flavorful dishes that reflect the country's agricultural history. Traditional Czech meals often include dishes like svíčková (marinated beef), goulash, and knedlíky (dumplings).

Culinary Customs:

Family Gatherings: Special occasions often involve large family gatherings where traditional Czech dishes are prepared and enjoyed together.

Festive Foods: Certain dishes, like vánoční cukroví (Christmas cookies), are associated with specific holidays and seasons.

Conclusion: Preserving Heritage Through Customs

These customs and traditions in the Czech Republic not only reflect the country's rich history but also contribute to a sense of community and cultural identity. Whether it's celebrating the changing seasons, partaking in festive rituals, or savoring traditional dishes, these customs weave a colorful tapestry that binds generations and preserves the unique heritage of the Czech people.

8.0 OUTDOOR ACTIVITIES

8.1 HIKING AND NATURE TRAILS

The Czech Republic, with its diverse landscapes and pristine nature, offers a plethora of hiking trails that cater to both avid hikers and casual nature enthusiasts. From lush forests and rolling hills to dramatic rock formations, these trails provide an immersive experience into the country's natural beauty. Here's an extensive exploration of some of the most captivating hiking and nature trails in the Czech Republic:

1. Bohemian Switzerland National Park: A Tapestry of Sandstone Formations
Location: Northern Bohemia

Description: Bohemian Switzerland, a national park renowned for its striking sandstone formations, offers a captivating hiking experience. The Pravčická brána, Europe's largest natural sandstone arch, is a highlight along with the picturesque Edmund Gorge.

Key Trails:
Gabriel's Trail: This trail takes you through the Pravčická brána and offers stunning views of the surrounding landscape.
Mikulášovy cesty: A series of trails leading through the diverse rock formations and lush forests of the park.

2. Šumava National Park: Wilderness in the Bohemian Forest
Location: Southwest Czech Republic

Description: Šumava National Park, the largest national park in the Czech Republic, is a haven for nature lovers. Hikers can explore dense forests, glacial lakes, and the Šumava Mountains, creating an enchanting landscape.

Highlighted Trails:

Poledník Lookout Trail: Leading to the Poledník peak, this trail provides panoramic views of the surrounding countryside.

Bohemian Forest Railway Trail: Following the historic railway route, this trail offers a journey through Šumava's diverse ecosystems.

3. Krkonoše National Park: Alpine Adventures in the Giant Mountains

Location: Northern Czech Republic

Description: The Krkonoše, or Giant Mountains, are the highest mountain range in the Czech Republic. The national park features alpine meadows, glacial cirques, and the highest peak, Sněžka. Hikers can explore diverse trails, ranging from gentle walks to challenging ascents.

Prominent Routes:

Sněžka Trail: A challenging ascent to the highest peak, rewarding hikers with panoramic views.

Czech-Polish Friendship Trail: Connecting the two countries, this trail offers a scenic trek through the heart of the Giant Mountains.

4. Adršpach-Teplice Rocks: Surreal Sandstone Labyrinths
Location: Northern Bohemia

Description: The Adršpach-Teplice Rocks are a mesmerizing labyrinth of sandstone formations, creating a surreal landscape. Hiking trails wind through towering rock pillars, deep crevices, and lush forested areas.

Unmissable Paths:
Grand Tour of Adršpach: A comprehensive trail that leads visitors through the most captivating rock formations in the area.
Teplice Rocks Trail: This trail explores the Teplice side, known for its unique sandstone sculptures.

5. Czech Paradise (Český ráj): Fairy-Tale Landscapes
Location: Northern Bohemia

Description: Czech Paradise is aptly named for its enchanting landscapes, characterized by sandstone formations, dense forests, and medieval castles. Hiking trails lead to iconic rock formations and viewpoints, providing a fairy-tale-like experience.

Signature Hikes:
Hruboskalsko Loop: This trail takes hikers through the iconic Hruboskalsko rock formations, offering panoramic views of the surrounding countryside.
Prachov Rocks Trail: Leading through the Prachov Rocks, this trail showcases towering sandstone towers and unique rock formations.

6. Jeseníky Mountains: Alpine Meadows and Serenity
Location: Northern Moravia

Description: The Jeseníky Mountains, often referred to as the "Roof of Moravia," boast alpine meadows, crystal-clear lakes, and expansive forests. Hiking trails cater to various skill levels, making it an ideal destination for both beginners and experienced hikers.

Memorable Routes:

Praděd Trail: Leading to the highest peak in the Jeseníky range, this trail offers stunning vistas and the iconic Praděd Tower.
Bílá Opava Trail: Following the Bílá Opava River, this trail meanders through serene landscapes and showcases the region's natural beauty.

7. Podyjí National Park: Riverside Trails and Vineyard Views
Location: Southern Moravia

Description: Podyjí National Park, situated along the Thaya River, is characterized by deep river valleys, picturesque meadows, and vineyards. Hiking trails along the riverbanks provide serene walks, and the park is known for its rich biodiversity.

Tranquil Paths:

Thaya Valley Trail: Following the meandering course of the Thaya River, this trail allows hikers to enjoy the tranquil beauty of Podyjí.
Hardegg Castle Trail: Connecting to Austria, this trail leads to Hardegg Castle, providing cross-border exploration.

8. Beskydy Mountains: Carpathian Charm and Cultural Heritage
Location: Eastern Czech Republic

Description: The Beskydy Mountains, part of the Carpathian range, offer a blend of natural beauty and cultural heritage. Hiking trails lead through dense forests, alpine meadows, and charming villages, allowing hikers to experience the traditional culture of the region.

Highlighted Routes:

Lysá Hora Trail: Leading to the highest peak in the Beskydy range, this trail offers panoramic views of the surrounding landscape.

Javorový Vrch Trail: Passing through traditional wooden architecture, this trail provides a glimpse into the cultural heritage of the Beskydy region.

9. Svatý Jan pod Skalou: Pilgrimage and Natural Wonders

Location: Central Bohemia

Description: Svatý Jan pod Skalou, or St. John under the Rock, is a pilgrimage site surrounded by picturesque

8.2 SKIING AND WINTER SPORTS

Czech Republic, with its picturesque landscapes and diverse topography, offers a fantastic playground for winter sports enthusiasts. While it might not be the first destination that comes to mind for skiing and winter sports, the country boasts several regions that cater to these activities, providing a unique and charming experience.

1. Mountainous Terrain:
The mountainous regions of the Czech Republic, particularly the Krkonoše Mountains, are a haven for winter sports. These mountains, the highest in the country, are home to several ski resorts, including Špindlerův Mlýn and Pec pod Sněžkou. The slopes here cater to various skill levels, making it an ideal destination for both beginners and experienced skiers.

2. Ski Resorts:
Špindlerův Mlýn, situated in the Krkonoše Mountains, is one of the most popular ski resorts in the Czech Republic. It offers a wide range of slopes, modern facilities, and a vibrant apres-ski scene. Other notable resorts include Harrachov and Lipno, each with its unique charm and amenities.

3. Cross-Country Skiing:
Beyond downhill skiing, the Czech Republic is renowned for its cross-country skiing trails. The Jizera Mountains, for example, feature an extensive network of trails suitable for

cross-country skiing, attracting enthusiasts who appreciate the serene beauty of the winter landscape.

4. Winter Events:
The Czech Republic hosts various winter sports events, attracting athletes and spectators from around the world. For instance, the Nordic Combined World Cup in Liberec and the FIS Cross-Country World Cup in Nove Mesto na Morave showcase the country's commitment to winter sports.

5. Charming Winter Villages:
The ambiance of Czech winter villages adds to the overall appeal of winter sports in the country. Traditional architecture, cozy accommodations, and local cuisine create an authentic and welcoming atmosphere for visitors.

6. Winter Hiking and Snowshoeing:
For those seeking alternatives to traditional skiing, the Czech Republic offers opportunities for winter hiking and snowshoeing. The Jeseníky

Mountains and Bohemian Forest provide breathtaking landscapes for these activities, allowing visitors to explore the winter wonderland at a more relaxed pace.

7. Accessibility:

The Czech Republic may not be the first name that comes to mind for winter sports, but it offers a delightful blend of diverse terrains, charming villages, and well-equipped resorts. Whether you are an avid skier, a fan of cross-country trails, or someone looking to explore winter activities beyond the slopes, the Czech Republic has something to offer for every winter sports enthusiast.

8.3 WATER ACTIVITIES

While the Czech Republic is often associated with its charming cities, historical sites, and picturesque landscapes, it also offers a variety of water activities thanks to its numerous rivers, lakes, and reservoirs. From leisurely cruises to adrenaline-pumping water sports, here's a closer look at the diverse water-based activities you can enjoy in the Czech Republic:

1. River Rafting and Kayaking:

The Czech Republic boasts several rivers that are perfect for rafting and kayaking adventures. The Vltava River, particularly the section near Český Krumlov, is a popular choice for both beginners and experienced paddlers. The Berounka River and the Otava River also offer scenic routes with varying levels of difficulty.

2. Canoeing:

Canoeing enthusiasts can explore the meandering rivers and picturesque landscapes that define the Czech countryside. The Sázava River, known for its calm waters and beautiful surroundings, is a favorite destination for canoe trips. It provides a relaxed setting for families and nature lovers to enjoy a day on the water.

3. Lakes and Reservoirs:

The Czech Republic is home to numerous lakes and reservoirs, providing opportunities for various water activities. Lipno Dam, the largest reservoir in the country, offers sailing, windsurfing, and fishing. Lake Mácha, surrounded by forests, is another popular spot for swimming, boating, and relaxation.

4. Houseboat Cruises:

Experience a unique water adventure by renting a houseboat and navigating through the country's waterways. The Vltava River and the Elbe River offer scenic routes for houseboat cruises, allowing you to enjoy the picturesque landscapes and charming villages along the banks.

5. Paddleboarding:

Paddleboarding has gained popularity in the Czech Republic, especially on the country's lakes and reservoirs. Whether you're a beginner or an experienced paddleboarder, the calm waters of lakes like Lipno provide an ideal setting for this relaxing water activity.

6. Fishing:

Fishing enthusiasts will find plenty of opportunities in the Czech Republic. The country's rivers and lakes are home to a variety of fish species, making it an attractive destination for anglers. Obtain the necessary permits and enjoy a peaceful day of fishing surrounded by nature.

7. Thermal Springs and Spas:

While not a traditional water activity, the Czech Republic is renowned for its thermal springs and spa culture. Towns like Karlovy Vary and Mariánské Lázně offer unique experiences, allowing visitors to relax in mineral-rich thermal waters known for their therapeutic properties.

8. Lakeside Relaxation:

Many lakes in the Czech Republic provide beautiful settings for a relaxing day by the water. Whether it's swimming, sunbathing, or enjoying a lakeside picnic, places like Lake Lipno and Lake Mácha offer a serene escape from the hustle and bustle of city life.

In conclusion, the Czech Republic's water activities cater to a diverse range of interests, from the thrill-seekers enjoying river rafting to those seeking relaxation by the tranquil lakeside. With its abundance of water bodies and stunning natural scenery, the country invites visitors to explore and embrace various aquatic adventures.

8.4 NATIONAL PARKS AND RESERVES

The Czech Republic is home to several stunning national parks and nature reserves, each offering a unique blend of natural beauty, diverse ecosystems, and opportunities for outdoor activities. These protected areas showcase the country's commitment to preserving its rich biodiversity and providing a haven for both wildlife and outdoor enthusiasts.

1. Šumava National Park:

Situated in the southwestern part of the country along the German border, Šumava National Park is the largest national park in the Czech Republic. Its vast expanse encompasses dense forests, peat bogs, and glacial lakes. Visitors can explore a network of hiking and cycling trails, immersing themselves in the park's pristine wilderness. The park is also home to rare species like the lynx and the black grouse.

2. Krkonoše National Park:

Nestled in the northeastern part of the country, Krkonoše National Park is known for its majestic mountains, including the highest peak in the Czech Republic, Sněžka. This park is a haven for hikers and winter sports enthusiasts, offering a network of trails, alpine meadows, and skiing opportunities during the winter months. The diverse flora and fauna, along with picturesque waterfalls, add to the park's allure.

3. Podyjí National Park:

Podyjí National Park, located along the Austrian border, is a unique blend of deep river valleys, meandering rivers, and untouched forests. The park is renowned for its biodiversity, and visitors can explore the landscape through hiking and cycling trails. The Thaya River, which flows through the park, creates a picturesque setting with its meanders and canyons.

4. Bohemian Switzerland National Park:

Bordering Germany, Bohemian Switzerland National Park is known for its dramatic sandstone formations, deep gorges, and lush forests. The iconic Pravčická brána, the largest natural sandstone arch in Europe, is a major attraction. Hiking trails lead visitors through this enchanting landscape, offering breathtaking views and encounters with diverse flora and fauna.

5. České Švýcarsko (Czech Switzerland):

While not a national park, České Švýcarsko, or Czech Switzerland, is a protected landscape area renowned for its sandstone rock formations and deep valleys. The Elbe Sandstone Mountains create a unique and visually striking environment, making it a paradise for rock climbers, hikers, and nature enthusiasts.

6. Protected Landscape Areas:

In addition to national parks, the Czech Republic has several protected landscape areas, such as Žďárské vrchy and Beskydy. These areas focus on preserving the natural and cultural heritage, featuring diverse ecosystems, historic landmarks, and traditional villages.

7. Wildlife Reserves:

Various wildlife reserves, like Bílé Karpaty and Třeboň, contribute to the conservation of native flora and fauna. These reserves aim to protect specific habitats, including wetlands and forests, fostering the survival of endangered species.

In summary, the Czech Republic's national parks and reserves showcase the country's dedication to preserving its natural treasures. Whether you're drawn to the rugged mountains, dense forests, or unique rock formations, these protected areas provide a wealth of opportunities for outdoor exploration, wildlife observation, and a deep connection with nature.

9.0 PRACTICAL TIPS

9.1 SAFETY AND EMERGENCY INFORMATION

Safety in the Czech Republic:

The Czech Republic is generally considered a safe destination for travelers. However, like any other country, it's essential to be aware of certain safety aspects to ensure a secure and enjoyable visit.

Low Crime Rates: The Czech Republic boasts relatively low crime rates compared to other European countries. Violent crimes are rare, and petty crimes such as pickpocketing may occur in crowded tourist areas, so it's advisable to stay vigilant in such places.

Public Transportation Safety: Public transportation in major cities, including Prague, is safe and efficient. However, be cautious of pickpockets, especially in crowded trams or buses. Use reputable taxi services or ride-sharing apps to avoid potential scams.

Healthcare Facilities: The Czech Republic has a well-developed healthcare system with modern facilities. European Union citizens can access medical services through the European Health Insurance Card (EHIC). Travelers from other countries should have comprehensive travel insurance that covers medical expenses.

Natural Hazards: The Czech Republic is not prone to natural disasters like earthquakes or hurricanes. However, travelers should be mindful of weather conditions, especially during winter when snow and icy conditions can affect road travel.

Emergency Information: In case of emergencies, knowing how to access help and support is crucial. Here is important emergency information for travelers in the Czech Republic:

Emergency Services:

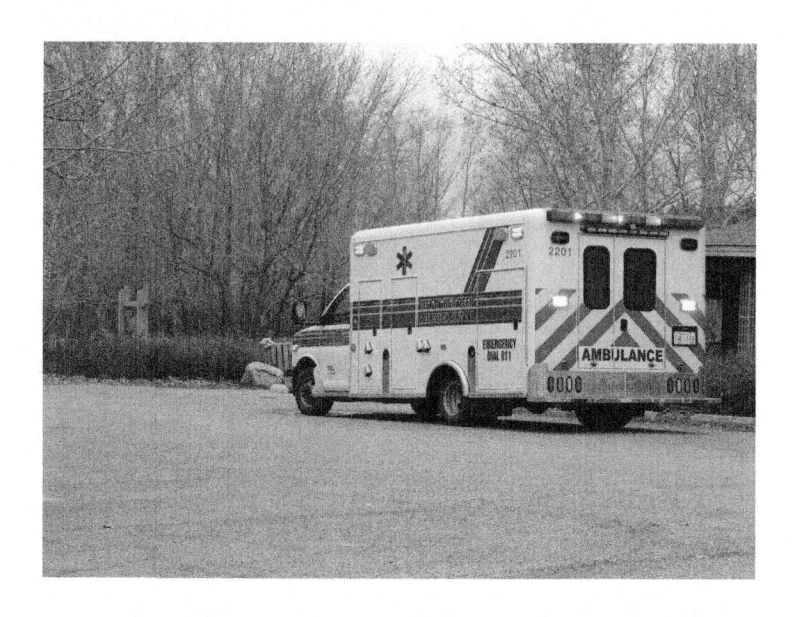

Police: 158

Medical Emergency: 155

Fire Department: 150

European Emergency Number: Dial 112 for a unified emergency number that connects to police, medical assistance, and fire services.

Embassy and Consulate Information: Locate the nearest embassy or consulate of your country. In Prague, many embassies are concentrated in the diplomatic district. Have the contact information readily available in case you need assistance.

Travel Insurance: Ensure you have comprehensive travel insurance covering medical emergencies, trip cancellations, and other unforeseen events. Keep a copy of your insurance policy and emergency contact numbers with you.

Language Barrier: While English is widely spoken, especially in tourist areas, it's helpful to know a few basic Czech phrases. In emergency situations, communication may be smoother if you can convey essential information.

Local Laws and Customs: Familiarize yourself with local laws and customs to avoid unintentional legal issues. Respect local customs and regulations, particularly when it comes to photography, behavior in religious sites, and alcohol consumption.

Safe Travel Practices: Secure your belongings in crowded areas.

Use official and reputable transportation services.

Be cautious with your personal information and belongings to prevent identity theft or fraud.

By staying informed and taking basic precautions, travelers can enjoy a safe and pleasant experience in the Czech Republic.

Always prioritize your well-being and be prepared to handle any unexpected situations that may arise during your visit.

9.2 HEALTH AND MEDICAL SERVICES

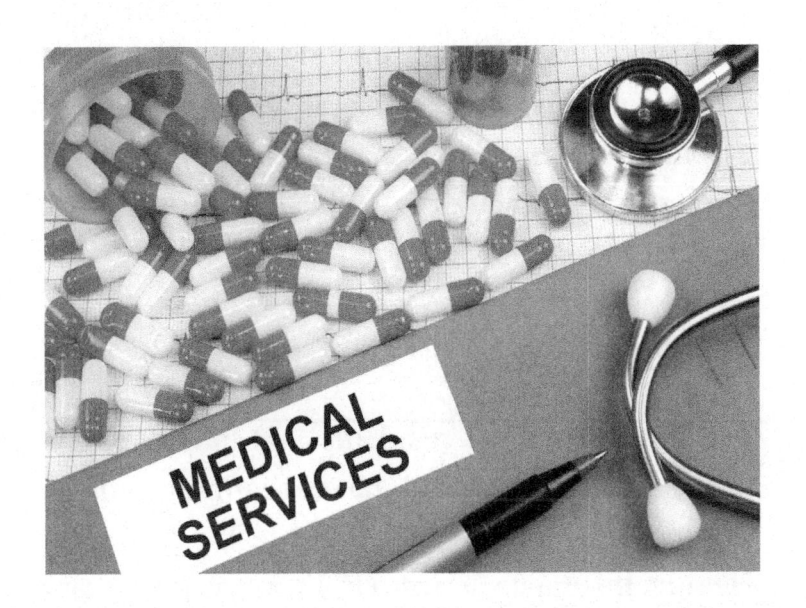

Healthcare System in the Czech Republic

The Czech Republic has a well-established healthcare system that provides accessible and high-quality medical services. Both residents and visitors can benefit from the country's comprehensive healthcare infrastructure.

1. Universal Healthcare

The Czech Republic operates under a universal healthcare system, ensuring that all residents and legally employed expatriates have access to essential medical services. This system is funded through mandatory health insurance contributions.

2. Health Insurance

It is mandatory for residents and employees in the Czech Republic to have health insurance. European Union citizens can use the European Health Insurance Card (EHIC) for necessary healthcare services. Non-EU citizens are advised to have comprehensive travel insurance to cover medical expenses.

3. Medical Facilities

Major cities in the Czech Republic, such as Prague, Brno, and Ostrava, are equipped with modern medical facilities, including hospitals, clinics, and specialized healthcare centers. These facilities meet international standards and offer a wide range of medical services.

4. General Practitioners and Specialists

Primary healthcare is provided by general practitioners (GP), who serve as the first point of contact for patients. Referrals to specialists are made when necessary, and the country has a diverse pool of medical specialists covering various fields.

5. Pharmacies

Pharmacies (lékárna) are widely available throughout the country, and many medications are accessible without a prescription. Pharmacists are knowledgeable and can provide advice on over-the-counter medications.

6. Emergency Services

In case of medical emergencies, dial the national emergency number 155. Ambulance services are prompt and efficient. Hospitals and emergency rooms are equipped to handle a range of medical situations.

7. Dental Care

Dental care is an integral part of the healthcare system. Many dentists in the Czech Republic speak English, and the country is known for providing quality dental services at reasonable prices.

8. English-Speaking Healthcare Professional

While Czech is the primary language, many healthcare professionals, especially in urban areas and tourist destinations, speak English. This ensures effective communication between healthcare providers and international patients.

9. Medical Tourism

The Czech Republic has become a popular destination for medical tourism, attracting visitors seeking specialized medical treatments and procedures. The country's medical facilities are equipped with state-of-the-art technology, and medical staff is highly trained.

10. COVID-19 Measures

During the global pandemic, the Czech Republic implemented various measures to curb the spread of COVID-19. This included widespread testing, vaccination campaigns, and public health guidelines.

11. Mental Health Services

Mental health services are available, and awareness of mental health issues is increasing. Psychiatric care is provided both in outpatient settings and within hospitals.

12. Alternative Medicine

The Czech Republic also embraces alternative and complementary medicine. Many healthcare facilities offer services such as acupuncture, herbal medicine, and homeopathy.

In conclusion, the Czech Republic's healthcare system is characterized by its accessibility, high standards, and a comprehensive range of services. Whether you are a resident or a visitor, you can expect reliable medical care and services that adhere to international standards.

9.3 LOCAL ETIQUETTE AND CUSTOMS

Understanding local etiquette and customs is crucial when visiting the Czech Republic to ensure respectful and positive interactions with the locals. Here are some key aspects of Czech etiquette and customs:

1. Greetings

- A firm handshake is the standard greeting in business and formal settings.
- Close friends and family often greet each other with a kiss on both cheeks.
- Address people using their titles and surnames unless invited to use their first name.

2. Punctuality

- Punctuality is generally expected in business and formal settings.
- Social events may have a more relaxed approach to timing, but it's still courteous to be reasonably prompt.

3. Table Manners

- Wait for the host to begin the meal and say "dobrou chut'" (good appetite) before starting to eat.

- Keep your hands on the table, but avoid putting your elbows on it.
- Finish everything on your plate as a sign of appreciation.

4. Tipping

- Tipping is customary in restaurants, and it is common to round up the bill or leave around 10% of the total.
- Tipping is also expected for good service in bars, cafes, and for services such as taxi rides.

5. Dress Code

- Czechs tend to dress more formally in business and formal settings.
- Casual attire is acceptable in most everyday situations, but it's advised to dress neatly and avoid overly casual clothing in formal environments.

6. Public Behavior

- Public behavior is generally reserved and polite.
- Keep conversations at a moderate volume, especially in public transportation and quiet areas.

7. Language

- While many Czechs speak English, particularly in urban areas, it's appreciated if you learn a few basic Czech phrases.
- Address people formally with titles and surnames until invited to use their first name.

8. Religion and Customs

- The Czech Republic is known for its religious diversity, and discussions about religion are often private matters.

- Respect religious customs and traditions, especially when visiting churches and religious sites.

9. Gifts

- When invited to someone's home, it's customary to bring a small gift, such as flowers, chocolates, or wine.
- Gifts are usually opened when received.

10. Shoes Indoors

- It's customary to take off your shoes when entering someone's home. This is a common practice to keep homes clean.

11. Cultural Sensitivity

- Be sensitive to the country's history, particularly regarding topics related to World War II and the Communist era.

- Avoid making jokes about Czech history and politics, as these topics can be sensitive.

12. Public Transportation

- Let passengers exit public transportation before entering.
- Priority seating is often reserved for seniors and pregnant women.

By being aware of and respecting these customs and etiquette guidelines, you'll contribute to a positive and culturally enriching experience while visiting the Czech Republic.

9.4 SUSTAINABLE TRAVEL PRACTICES

Sustainable travel practices are essential to minimize the environmental and cultural impact of tourism. When visiting the Czech Republic or any destination, consider incorporating these sustainable travel practices:

Respect Local Wildlife and Nature

Stay on marked trails to avoid disturbing wildlife and damaging vegetation.

Refrain from feeding animals in natural habitats.

Choose Eco-Friendly Accommodations

Opt for hotels, guesthouses, or hostels that have eco-friendly practices, such as energy-saving initiatives and waste reduction.

Conserve Water and Energy

- Use water and energy resources responsibly. Turn off lights, air conditioning, and heating when leaving your accommodation.
- Reuse towels and linens to minimize laundry and conserve water.

Support Local Businesses

- Choose locally owned hotels, restaurants, and shops to contribute to the local economy.
- Purchase souvenirs made by local artisans, supporting traditional craftsmanship.

Reduce Single-Use Plastics

- Bring a reusable water bottle and fill it from taps or water fountains.
- Say no to single-use plastics, such as straws and plastic bags, and opt for reusable alternatives.

Use Public Transportation and Walk

- Utilize public transportation to reduce your carbon footprint.
- Walk or bike when exploring cities or natural areas to minimize environmental impact.

7. Minimize Waste

- Avoid excessive packaging by bringing a reusable shopping bag and saying no to unnecessary packaging.
- Dispose of waste responsibly by using designated recycling bins.

8. Learn About and Respect Local Culture

- Familiarize yourself with local customs, traditions, and etiquette to show respect for the host culture.
- Support cultural heritage sites and learn about their preservation efforts.

Participate in Conservation Activities

- Join organized clean-up or conservation projects during your visit.
- Contribute to local environmental initiatives or volunteer with conservation organizations.

Choose Sustainable Tours and Activities

- Opt for eco-friendly tours that prioritize environmental and cultural preservation.

- Participate in activities that promote wildlife conservation and responsible interactions with animals.

Conserve Energy in Your Accommodation

- Turn off lights, electronics, and air conditioning when not in use.
- Adjust your thermostat to conserve energy and reduce your environmental impact.

Offset Your Carbon Emissions

- Consider carbon offset programs to compensate for your travel-related emissions.
- Support initiatives that focus on reforestation and renewable energy projects.

Educate Yourself and Others

- Stay informed about sustainable travel practices and share this knowledge with fellow travelers.
- Encourage others to adopt eco-friendly habits and contribute to sustainable tourism.

By incorporating these sustainable travel practices, you can minimize your environmental footprint, support local communities, and contribute to the preservation of the cultural and natural heritage of the Czech Republic and other destination.

10.0 USEFUL RESOURCES

10.1 ESSENTIAL APPS AND WEBSITES

When traveling to the Czech Republic, there are several essential apps and websites that can enhance your experience, from navigation to language assistance and local information:

1. Google Maps

Google Maps

Navigate through cities, find attractions, and plan your routes using Google Maps. It provides real-time directions for walking, driving, and public transportation.

2. Duolingo or Google Translate

Learn basic Czech phrases with language learning apps like Duolingo. Google Translate can also be handy for translating text or speech in real-time.

3. Czech Railways (České dráhy) App

If you plan to explore the country by train, the Czech Railways app provides information on train schedules, ticket prices, and platform details.

4. IDOS

IDOS is a comprehensive transportation app for the Czech Republic, offering information on buses, trams, and trains, including schedules and routes.

5. WhatsApp or Messenger

Stay connected with locals and fellow travelers using popular messaging apps like WhatsApp or Messenger. Many locals prefer these platforms for communication.

6. Visit Czech Republic (Official Tourism App)

The official tourism app provides information on attractions, events, and practical travel tips for various cities in the Czech Republic.

7. Currency Converter Apps

XE Currency or any reliable currency converter app can help you convert prices to your home currency and manage your budget effectively.

8. HappyCow

If you have dietary preferences or restrictions, HappyCow is a useful app to find vegetarian, vegan, and vegetarian-friendly restaurants in the Czech Republic.

9. WiFi Map

Access free WiFi hotspots using WiFi Map. It provides a map of available WiFi networks, which can be especially useful for staying connected on the go.

10. Weather Apps

Check the weather forecast with apps like AccuWeather or Weather.com to plan your activities and pack accordingly.

11. WhatsApp or Viber

These messaging apps are widely used for both local and international communication. You can make calls and send messages over Wi-Fi to avoid roaming charges.

12. Airbnb or Booking.com

Use accommodation apps like Airbnb or Booking.com to find and book hotels, hostels, or private accommodations.

13. Yelp or TripAdvisor

Discover restaurants, attractions, and reviews using apps like Yelp or TripAdvisor to make informed decisions during your travels.

14. Emergency Apps

Save local emergency numbers on your phone and consider installing safety apps that provide real-time information about potential risks and emergencies.

Remember to download these apps before your trip to ensure you have access to information, maps, and translation services even when offline. Having these tools at your fingertips will contribute to a smoother and more enjoyable experience in the Czech Republic.

10.2 RECOMMENDED GUIDEBOOKS

Guidebooks can be invaluable resources for travelers, providing insights into local culture, history, attractions, and practical travel tips. Here are some recommended guidebooks for exploring the Czech Republic:

Lonely Planet Czech Republic

Lonely Planet is known for its detailed and well-researched travel guides. The Czech

Republic edition covers everything from historical sites to local cuisine and includes maps for easy navigation.

Rick Steves Prague & The Czech Republic

Rick Steves' guidebooks are popular for their practical advice and cultural insights. This guide covers not only Prague but also delves into other regions of the Czech Republic.

DK Eyewitness Travel Guide: Czech and Slovak Republics

The DK Eyewitness guides are known for their visual appeal, with stunning photographs, illustrations, and detailed maps. This guide covers both the Czech and Slovak Republics, providing a comprehensive overview.

Rough Guide to the Czech Republic

Rough Guides offer a mix of practical information and cultural insights. This guide to the Czech Republic includes detailed coverage of cities, towns, and outdoor activities.

National Geographic Traveler: Prague and the Czech Republic

National Geographic guides are known for their high-quality photography and cultural focus. This guide provides in-depth information about Prague and the surrounding regions.

Bradt Guide to the Czech Republic

The Bradt guides are often praised for their in-depth coverage of destinations. This guide to the Czech Republic offers detailed information on lesser-known attractions and cultural nuances.

Fodor's Essential Czech Republic

Fodor's guidebooks provide comprehensive information for various travel styles. The

Essential Czech Republic guide includes recommendations for accommodation, dining, and activities.

Insight Guides: Explore Prague

Insight Guides focus on specific cities or regions. "Explore Prague" provides detailed information about the capital city's attractions, history, and local culture.

Moon Prague, Vienna & Budapest

Moon Travel Guides are known for their emphasis on unique and local experiences. This guide covers not only Prague but also Vienna and Budapest, making it suitable for travelers exploring multiple cities.

Berlitz Pocket Guide Czech Republic:

Berlitz Pocket Guides are compact and easy to carry. This guide offers concise information on top attractions, activities, and essential travel tips.

Before choosing a guidebook, consider your travel preferences, interests, and the level of detail you desire. Some travelers prefer comprehensive guides, while others may opt for more condensed versions. Additionally, check for the most recent editions to ensure the information is up-to-date.

10.3 LOCAL TOURIST INFORMATION CENTERS

When visiting the Czech Republic, you can find tourist information centers in various cities and tourist destinations. These centers are valuable resources for obtaining maps, brochures, and up-to-date information about local attractions, events, and services. Here are examples of tourist information centers in some prominent cities:

Prague

Prague City Tourism Information Centers are located at strategic points throughout the city, including Old Town Square, Prague Castle, and the main train station. The main office is at the Old Town Hall (Staroměstská radnice).

Brno

Tourist Information Centre Brno is situated in the heart of the city, near the Vegetable Market (Zelný trh). It provides information about Brno's attractions, events, and accommodations.

Český Krumlov

Český Krumlov Information Centre is centrally located in the historic town and offers information about the UNESCO-listed site, including castle tours, river cruises, and local events.

Karlovy Vary

The Information Centre Karlovy Vary is in the main spa area and provides details about the city's famous thermal springs, spa treatments, and cultural events.

Plzeň

Plzeň Tourist Information Centre is located in the city center near the Pilsner Urquell Brewery. It offers information about the city's breweries, historic sites, and events.

Olomouc

Tourist Information Centre Olomouc is situated in the heart of the city on Horní náměstí (Upper Square). It provides information about

Olomouc's historical landmarks and cultural activities.

Kutná Hora

The Tourist Information Centre in Kutná Hora is located near the historical center and offers details about the city's UNESCO-listed sites, including the Sedlec Ossuary and St. Barbara's Church.

Ostrava

Ostrava Tourist Information Centre is in the city center, providing information about Ostrava's industrial heritage, cultural events, and outdoor activities.

Liberec

Liberec Tourist Information Centre is located in the city center and offers information about attractions like Ještěd Tower, Liberec Zoo, and local museums.

České Budějovice

České Budějovice Tourist Information Centre is situated near the city center and provides information about the historical sites, including the famous Budweiser Brewery.

These are just a few examples, and you can find tourist information centers in many other cities and tourist destinations throughout the Czech Republic. These centers typically offer assistance in multiple languages and can help you make the most of your visit by providing maps, brochures, and personalized recommendations.

11.0 APPENDIX

11.1 GLOSSARY OF CZECH PHRASES

Sure, here's a glossary of basic Czech phrases that can be useful during your visit:

Greetings and Politeness

Hello - Ahoj (informal), Dobrý den (formal)

Good morning - Dobré ráno

Good afternoon - Dobré odpoledne

Good evening - Dobrý večer

Goodbye - Na shledanou

Please - Prosím

Thank you - Děkuji

Excuse me - S dovolením (when asking to pass), Promiňte (when apologizing)

Common Expressions

Yes - Ano

No - Ne

Maybe - Možná

I don't understand - Nerozumím

Do you speak English? - Mluvíte anglicky?

I'm sorry - Omlouvám se

What is your name? - Jak se jmenujete? (formal), Jak se jmenuješ? (informal)

My name is... - Jmenuji se...

Directions

Where is...? - Kde je...?

Left - Vlevo

Right - Vpravo

Straight ahead - Rovně

Map - Mapa

Numbers

One - Jeden

Two - Dva

Three - Tři

Four - Čtyři

Five - Pět

Ten - Deset

Shopping and Dining

How much does it cost? - Kolik to stojí?

I would like... - Chtěl bych... (male), Chtěla bych... (female)

Menu - Jídelníček

Water - Voda

Beer - Pivo

Coffee - Káva

Bill, please - Účet, prosím

Emergency Phrases:

Help! - Pomoc!

I need a doctor - Potřebuji doktora

Where is the hospital? - Kde je nemocnice?

Police - Policie

I've lost my... - Ztratil(a) jsem svůj/svou...

Time and Dates:

What time is it? - Kolik je hodin?

Today - Dnes

Tomorrow - Zítra

Yesterday - Včera

Monday - Pondělí

January - Leden

June - Červen (months are often referred to by color in Czech)

Feel free to use this glossary as a quick reference during your travels in the Czech Republic. Learning a few basic phrases can enhance your experience and interactions with locals.

11.2 MAPS AND NAVIGATIONAL AIDS

Navigating a new destination is made significantly easier with the help of maps and navigational aids. In the Czech Republic, you can use various tools to ensure you find your way around efficiently. Here are some recommended maps and navigational aids:

1. Google Maps

Google Maps is a versatile and widely used mapping tool. It provides real-time navigation for walking, driving, and public transportation. Download offline maps for areas with limited connectivity.

2. IDOS

IDOS is a comprehensive public transportation app specific to the Czech Republic. It offers information about trains, buses, and trams, including schedules and routes.

3. Mapy.cz:

Mapy.cz is a popular Czech mapping application. It offers detailed maps, hiking and cycling trails, and points of interest. It can be particularly useful for outdoor activities.

4. Prague Metro and Tram Map

If you are exploring Prague, having a metro and tram map specific to the city is handy. These maps are available online and at metro stations.

5. GPS Navigation & Maps Sygic

Sygic is a navigation app that allows you to download offline maps, making it useful in areas with no internet connection. It provides turn-by-turn voice navigation.

6. Uber or Bolt

For convenient and reliable rides within cities, consider using ride-sharing apps like Uber or Bolt.

7. CzechTourism Official App

The CzechTourism app offers maps, information about tourist attractions, and events throughout the country. It can be a helpful resource for planning your itinerary.

8. HERE WeGo

HERE WeGo is another excellent navigation app that allows you to download maps for offline use. It provides directions for walking, driving, and public transportation.

9. Waze

Waze is a community-driven navigation app that provides real-time traffic updates, road conditions, and alternative routes. It's beneficial for driving in both cities and rural areas.

10. Signs and Wayfinding

Pay attention to road signs, especially when driving. Many signs in tourist areas are also in English, but familiarizing yourself with common road signs can be helpful.

11. Offline Travel Guides

Consider downloading offline travel guides or eBooks for the Czech Republic. These may include detailed maps, historical information, and practical tips.

12. Pocket Earth:

Pocket Earth is an offline mapping app that allows you to download detailed maps and plan routes without an internet connection.

Before your trip, ensure you download necessary maps and apps, especially if you plan to explore areas with limited internet connectivity. Having a combination of online and offline navigational aids will help you navigate the Czech Republic confidently.

11.3 WEATHER AND CLIMATE INFORMATION

Czech Republic map of Köppen climate classification

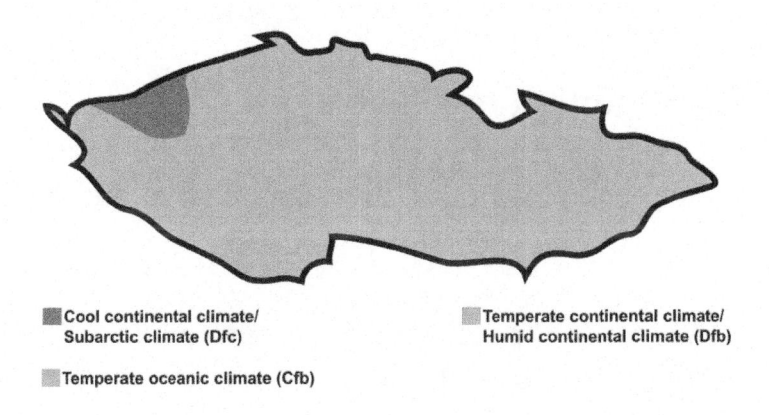

■ Cool continental climate/ Subarctic climate (Dfc)
■ Temperate continental climate/ Humid continental climate (Dfb)
■ Temperate oceanic climate (Cfb)

The weather in the Czech Republic varies across seasons, offering distinct experiences for travelers. Here's a general overview of the country's weather and climate:

1. Spring (March to May)

Spring brings milder temperatures, ranging from 10°C to 20°C (50°F to 68°F).

Blooming flowers and blossoming trees create a picturesque landscape.

It's a great time for outdoor activities, exploring cities, and enjoying the countryside.

2. Summer (June to August)

Summer is warm, with temperatures ranging from 20°C to 30°C (68°F to 86°F).

This is the peak tourist season, with longer daylight hours and various cultural events and festivals.

Ideal for hiking, outdoor festivals, and exploring historical sites.

3. Autumn (September to November)

Autumn brings cooler temperatures, ranging from 10°C to 20°C (50°F to 68°F).

The fall foliage creates a colorful backdrop, making it a scenic time to visit.

It's a good season for wine enthusiasts as grape harvesting takes place.

4. Winter (December to February)

Winters are cold, with temperatures often ranging from -5°C to 5°C (23°F to 41°F).

Snowfall is common, especially in higher elevations and mountainous regions.

Winter sports enthusiasts can enjoy skiing and snowboarding in popular areas like Špindlerův Mlýn and Harrachov.

Additional Weather Tips

The weather can vary between regions and elevations. Mountainous areas tend to be cooler than lowland regions.

Be prepared for sudden weather changes, especially in mountainous regions.

Check the specific weather forecast for the region you plan to visit, as conditions can differ.

Best Time to Visit

The best time to visit depends on your preferences. Spring and autumn are generally pleasant with fewer crowds, while summer is bustling with cultural events and festivals.

Winter is ideal for those who enjoy winter sports or want to experience a festive holiday season.

Average Temperature in Prague

Summer: 20°C to 30°C (68°F to 86°F)

Autumn: 10°C to 20°C (50°F to 68°F)

Winter: -5°C to 5°C (23°F to 41°F)

Spring: 10°C to 20°C (50°F to 68°F)

Remember to check the weather forecast closer to your travel dates for more accurate and specific information. Whether you're exploring historic cities, hiking in the countryside, or hitting the slopes, the Czech Republic offers diverse experiences throughout the year.

Printed in Great Britain
by Amazon